MW01113823

A Practical Guide for Personal Ministry

empowered

PAM PALAGYI

Empowered: A Practical Guide for Personal Ministry

Copyright © 2015 Pam Palagyi

ISBN 978-1-945084-01-0

www.pampalagyi.com

Unless otherwise indicated, all Scripture quotations are taken from The Holy Bible, New International Version. Copyright © 1973, 1978, 1984 by International Bible Society.

Published by Arise Publishing

DEDICATION

This book is dedicated to my family. First, to my husband Paul, daughters Lisa and Laurie and their families whose love has always been a source of strength and encouragement to me. Second, to my greater church family and the many friends who support my efforts.

FORWARD

Empowered is a book that is informative, innovative and instructional. Using biblical concepts, it makes the unseen realm both visible and tangible...like the author.

Pam Palagyi is a living example of this life style that is demonstrated in the many hats she wears both daily and seasonal. She is a wife, mother, church leader, mentor, ministry team player. As a daughter of the King of Kings, she is sharing with us an example of a life that is "empowered". Since meeting Pam and her husband Paul, it was always evident that her desire and passion is to see the Kingdom of God advancing in other people's life and calling.

Because we are living in perilous times (2 Timothy 3 NKJV), many Believers must be empowered and activated in our faith. Light and darkness are increasing (Isaiah 60:1-5) and we must not only be connected and empowered to Him, but with those who are like-minded.

Pam lays out five steps for effective ministry: knowledge, confidence, action, habits and success. Reading the book will be spiritually invigorating and rejuvenating. All who desire to be students of "The Way"and instructed in the Kingdom of God should have it in their library.

Personally knowing the person, Pam has ignited a flame to be prayerful, to be prepared, to be ready and stay faithful. As we grow in grace and knowledge and increase our spiritual understanding on the spiritual gifts, the blood of Christ and all of the tools we have to co-labor with Him, we can answer his call. Not only will we discover "what's in it for us"? but also, "what's in it for God"?

~ Aaron Evans

THE EMERGING DANIEL COMPANY INT'L

TABLE OF CONTENTS

INTRODUCTION

As a former Camp Fire Girl, I built more than my fair share of fires. I remember the many twigs, sticks, and logs laid one upon another in some "tepee" or "log cabin" shape. From the littlest of branches to the larger limbs, each piece had its place in starting the fire. If I arranged the twigs correctly, I only needed one match to ignite the entire pile. In a matter of minutes, the dry stack of wood became a blazing inferno.

Amazingly, I have seen God use the same technique in his church. In this case, however, the sticks that make up the fire are not pieces of wood, but Biblical concepts. When knowledge, understanding, and faith combine, it only takes one touch from the hand of God. A single spark from heaven ignites the spiritual fire within us!

Empowered offers both the raw material and the flint to ignite the spiritual flame. The text is a compilation of the many seminars and training sessions I have led over the years. I have already used the concepts found within these pages to train church teams, ministries, and traveling collegiate groups. They are effective in a variety of settings, age groups, and cultures.

As the second book in the **Foundations of Faith** series, *Empowered* equips the reader with fundamental Biblical concepts that lead to active ministry. I designed the book for use in one of two ways.

First, it provides a solid foundation for the training of altar workers. I use this term to describe those designated by their respective churches to pray for others during ministry times.

Second, it is an introduction to practical ministry for every Christian who wants to be used by God. To those who hunger to see the power of God in their everyday lives, this book supplies the basic knowledge for activating that desire.

How to Use This Book

Empowered fits many different settings and uses. The format works for individuals, small groups, Bible studies, or ministry teams. Each chapter can be followed by prayer and practical exercises found in the study guide. All of these practices work together to activate the group or individual. He or she is now equipped to operate in various ministry situations.

It is my hope that *Empowered* will advance the kingdom of God by preparing believers to act on their faith. My heart's desire is to see the Church equipped, prepared, and fully functioning at its highest level of excellence. Whether ministry occurs within the church, in the marketplace, or community, God is ready to touch lives and transform people!

Chapter 1
KINDLING THE DESIRE

God is on the move!

We live in a day and hour where the power of God is flowing as never before. He is transforming people, families, and entire nations at an accelerated pace.

The clock is ticking. God is looking for anyone who is willing to be a part of this dynamic movement. He is calling out to his people to join him in an unprecedented flow of power and anointing.

Will you play a part in this sovereign plan?

Are you ready to burn with the fire of God?

Do you long to see his power become a reality in your church, marketplace, and community?

If the answer to any of these questions is a resounding

YES, get ready to move beyond the ordinary and into the extraordinary. God is waiting for you to take part in this surge of his power. It's time to activate your faith and be empowered for ministry!

You may be asking "why me?" I'm just an ordinary Christian. Isn't that the job of the pastor?

God chose every Christian to carry his presence. We have each been given power, authority, and spiritual gifts to reach out to a hurting world. We are his representatives, his ambassadors here on earth. Whenever we minister in his name, we act on his behalf. Because he made us in his image, we have the right and privilege to do the works of God.

Jesus put it this way and told his disciples:

> *I tell you the truth, anyone who has faith*
> *in me will do what I have been doing. He will*
> *do even greater things than these, because I*
> *am going to the Father. (John 14:12)*

"Anyone" means young or old, new Christian or seasoned believer. It doesn't matter if you have a seminary degree or attend children's church. You have the power to touch the lives of others with God's holy power.

Jesus also stated that signs and wonders would follow the preaching of his word! (Mark 16:15-18) Can we trust him that he meant what he said? Will Jesus really back up what he promised?

The records of the early church witnessed countless miracles, healings, deliverances, and salvations. And these were not associated exclusively with the apostles!

• Philip was a man who heard God's voice, obeyed his command to speak to an Ethiopian eunuch. He led him to salvation and water baptism. (Acts 8:26-40)

• Stephen was a disciple *full of God's grace and power...doing great wonders and miraculous signs among the people.* (Acts 6:8)

Both of these men served as deacons, not the pastoral leaders of the church in Jerusalem. They had been chosen to wait on tables and distribute food to the widows. But their ministry extended beyond meeting the physical needs of the early church. They entered into a dynamic realm of service to God.

Christ has not changed in 2000 years—He is the same yesterday, today, and forever. His power and authority have not diminished. His promise to empower the early disciples is still viable for us today. The life of a 21st century Christian should be characterized by a confident ability to do the works of Jesus!

So, how do we begin to move in that direction? How do we willing participate and develop the practical aspects of ministry?

Connected and Empowered

From Genesis to Revelation, God has always wanted connection and intimacy with his people. He wooed Adam and Eve in the Garden of Eden. He dwelt among the Israelites in the Tabernacle of Moses. Jesus lived his life among the Jews. And at the end of the Bible, God promises to once again reside in the midst of his people.

Connection and empowerment are two sides of the same coin. If we connect to God, his power will flow through us to others. Conversely, power is the product of a vibrant relationship with God. This is the beginning and foundation of all ministry.

We act in cooperation with what heaven already wants to do. When we walk closely with God, we begin to recognize his prompting and respond. We become his hands and feet on earth, a channel of his goodness towards others. Without him, we can do nothing:

I am the vine; you are the branches…If you remain in me and my words remain in you, ask whatever you wish, and it will be done for you. (John 15:5-7)

Peter and John understood the power and authority given to them. They knew their assignment. One day as they approached the temple, they saw a man lame from birth at the gate called Beautiful. Peter spoke these words to the cripple: *Silver and gold I do not have, but what I do have I give you.* Peter took him by the hand, helped him up, and the man walked, jumped, and praised God. (Acts 3:1-10)

When we connect to God, we become sensitive to the way he operates. We begin to see with his eyes, hear with his ears, and act with his hands.

In my experience, I have seen God respond to three things…faith, need, and expectation. When any or all of these are present, God is ready to act.

Faith is an important concept, a necessary component of effective prayer. *It is the confidence of what we hope for and the assurance of what we do not see.* (Hebrews 11:1)

Jesus told Jairus, the synagogue leader, not to be afraid. Even though his daughter was dead and the situation looked hopeless, Christ's words to Jairus were, *Don't be afraid; just believe.* (Mark 5:35) He would speak those same words to us today...just believe!

Some say that the person receiving ministry must reach a certain level of faith before they can receive from God. But that viewpoint does not agree with scripture.

In Mark Chapter 2, it was the faith of a few friends that prompted them to lower their sick companion through the roof. Many came to Jesus believing he could heal, but sometimes it was Christ's faith that activated the power of God. Faith is an essential part of the process, but it is not limited to the one receiving ministry.

And without faith it is impossible to please God, because anyone who comes to him must believe that he exists and that he rewards those who earnestly seek him. (Hebrews 11:6)

God also responds to **Need**. There have been times when my presence and ministry are an answer to someone's prayer. A mother or father may have asked God for intervention, and I found myself as the vehicle that provided God's reply.

When I worked as a tutor, I was called to assist a young man who was flunking his freshman year of high school. It was Spring and he had just broken his leg in a skiing accident. My assignment was to help him complete the school year.

Although nothing was ever said, I sensed that his mother had prayed desperately for an answer to the dilemma. God answered by sending me. In just two months, God reversed the situation in a miraculous way. The young man finished his freshman year with A's and B's and went on to be very successful in high school and then college. The compassionate heart of God responded to the need and the heartfelt cry of a mother.

Finally, **Expectation** is the third component which triggers a response from God. When someone asks for prayer, they come anticipating a touch from God. Their expectant hope becomes the connecting point to the power of God. It elicits a reaction and he moves on their behalf.

During times of ministry, I have seen firsthand the difference that expectation makes. Those who come for a spiritual touch with high expectations, are much more likely to receive from God. Their confidence becomes the bridge that joins the natural to the supernatural realm.

And I pray that you…may be filled to the measure of all the fullness of God…who is able to do immeasurably more than all we ask or imagine, according to his power that is at work within us…(Ephesians 3:17-20)

Connection to God is the basis for all ministry. It makes us sensitive to his leading and empowers us to act. The Apostle Paul instructed the church to *be filled with the Spirit.* (Ephesians 5:18) The verb tense here actually means to be continually filled. Once is not enough. We must continue to be full, an overflow and connection that will impact the lives of others.

The Pathway to Power!

As we prepare to launch into the supernatural realm, we will start at the very beginning. Let's examine five distinct steps which are a road map to effective ministry.

We all start in a place of ignorance. Quite often, we just don't know what we don't know. But as we begin to master those spiritual concepts, we build a foundation and gain confidence to move forward. With each successive step, we move towards a lifestyle of active and powerful service.

1. Knowledge. This is the first step. We begin by recognizing that we are somewhat ignorant! It's not that God's ways are complex; they are simple. But sometimes we need instruction because the kingdom of heaven functions differently than the world in which we live.

In the natural realm, we know that if an apple drops from the tree and hits the ground, it illustrates the Law of Gravity. But do we recognize that although they are unseen, God has created spiritual forces and that are also at work?

Many of us have not grown up in a Christian culture where the power of God is normal; it is not second nature to us. Discovering true spiritual knowledge reveals possibilities that were foreign to us. Sparks begin to fly!

If this is new to you, don't be discouraged. Even the first disciples needed training. They lived alongside Jesus for a period of over three years. During this time, they grew to understand the "who," "what," "when," "where," and "why" of service to their Lord. Not only did Jesus teach them, but he allowed them to gain hands-on experience along the way. They observed. They ministered. They grew. Knowledge laid the foundation for their future actions in ministry. They understood who they were in relationship to Christ.

For several years, I trained traveling teams for a collegiate Christian ministry. Each weekend, these teams traveled across the Southeast preaching, leading worship, and inviting their audience to respond to the message. The ministry team would then pray for those specific needs.

After one training seminar, I had the opportunity to observe the group at a local youth outreach. The ministry was amazing! The students didn't hesitate to boldly pray with power and authority. Many were saved, received the Baptism of the Holy Spirit, and were healed. The training had catapulted these young men and women into a new dimension of ministry. They were confident of their ability and position in Christ.

In addition to the nuts and bolts of practical knowledge, we must also "know" our Lord. We must become familiar with his nature and his word which dictates his will. We may need to ask ourselves the familiar question, "What would Jesus do?" How can we answer, if we aren't familiar with the compassionate nature of our Lord? As we grow in understanding and the knowledge of him, we will gain insight into his ways.

2. Confidence. The second step is confidence. The practical and spiritual knowledge we gain gives us the courage to step out of the proverbial boat.

Remember Peter's experience walking on the water? He had seen the miracles of Jesus and was confident of Christ's power to uphold him on the waves. Yes, Peter took his eyes off Jesus and began to sink, but he was the one disciple who ventured out of the boat and actually did defy natural law. Peter actually walked on the water!

As we develop confidence in who we are and what God has invited us to do, we are no longer wondering whether we should or even could offer spiritual assistance. We become assured of what we know, and now have the certainty to proceed forward. Our faith is energized and that confidence produces action.

3. Action. With a foundation of knowledge and confidence, we become Christians in motion, active for the Kingdom of God. We are able to pray with others whenever and wherever the Holy Spirit prompts us.

Ministry isn't always confined to a church setting. In fact, God is on the move within our community, workplace, school, and neighborhood.

One day in Border's bookstore, I was simply sipping coffee and flipping through a magazine to pass the time. A young lady sitting to my left began to share about an upcoming operation, and I could tell she was distressed.

I used the opportunity to pray with her and asked for God's peace to surround the situation. The effect was immediate. He was faithful to answer my prayer and respond to her need. I left Border's encouraged by the fact that God had used me. She walked away knowing there is a God who loves and cares about her every need.

As we become more in tune with our Heavenly Father and his will, our actions become consistent and reliable. We move from the active phase into the fourth step. Consistent actions produce positive habits.

4. Habits. This fourth step is a result of faithfully responding to God over a period of time. It generally takes about six weeks of consistent behavior for any new physical action to become a habit.

Spiritual habits are developed in a similar fashion. With commitment and practice, our ministry habits will last a lifetime and touch the lives of countless hurting people.

Consider how a sprinter trains. The runner exercises and develops his muscles, practices his starting stance, and perfects his running strategy for the upcoming race. When the starting gun sounds, he doesn't hesitate or fumble off the blocks, but moves smoothly into the actions he has trained his body to perform. It has become second nature to him.

As representatives of God, our actions should

become second nature as well. Of course there will be challenges, missed opportunities, or seeming "failures" as part of the learning process, but it is habits...good habits performed over a lifetime...that birth the final step. We all desire to be successful!

5. *Success.* Jesus has sent us into this world to make disciples, pray for the sick, and deliver the oppressed. Success in the eyes of God embodies these characteristics. At the end of our lives, we all want to hear, "Well done, good and faithful servant!"

Ministry is no longer limited to the church and the altar. God is at work in neighborhoods, job sites, schools, and anywhere the Holy Spirit finds a need. Allow the following pages to equip, guide, and assure you that you have a place in God's plan.

He wants to use YOU!

Chapter 2
POSITIONED FOR POWER

As we begin to explore the "how to's" of ministry, our journey starts in the Old Testament. It is here that we uncover the spiritual roots that will prepare and position us for powerful prayer ministry.

God established divine patterns and procedures early on with his people. The Patriarchs Abraham, Isaac, and Jacob understood the fundamentals of approaching God. They offered sacrifices at altars and met with God there.

However, God developed a formal priesthood during the time of Moses. With the building of the Tabernacle, God began to interact directly with the masses through these specific men chosen to fulfill that role.

Three key spiritual elements...the priest, the altar, and the sacrifice...pave the way for our understanding

27

of ministry. These concepts illustrate not only the purpose, but provide the scriptural basis for effective modern-day ministry.

The Person...The Priest

But you are a chosen people, a royal priesthood, a holy nation, a people belonging to God, that you may declare the praises of him who called you out of darkness into his wonderful light. (1 Peter 2:9)

The priesthood began in Genesis with the Patriarchs. Each man stood before God in his own behalf or for his family. There was direct communication between God and his spiritual leaders.

In the Book of Exodus, priests were selected and set apart from the general population. Their duty and service centered on God. In order to prepare for their ministry, priests were ceremonially washed with water, anointed with oil, and dressed in holy garments to distinguish their role. They performed a two-fold function. These men represented the people before God and they represented God to the people.

As part of their service, Levitical priests offered sacrifices for themselves, the nation, and individuals. They helped others bring their offerings before God in the ways he had designated. These Old Testament ministers acted as a liaison. They became a practical touch-point that ushered people into a divine interaction with God.

Priests also ministered in the veiled inner court of the Tabernacle. Beyond sight of the people, they represented all of Israel as they fulfilled their duties before God.

As his children, God has chosen us as New Testament, modern-day priests. 1 Peter 2:9 calls us a *holy priesthood*. Whether we stand at a formal church altar or out in our communities ready to serve, we enter into the spiritual duties of a priest.

Like those of old, we too have a dual obligation. We come before God and our focus is vertical— we minister unto God and commune with him on a personal level. And, like the priests of old, our focus is also horizontal—we minister in behalf of God, taking the provision of Christ's work at Calvary out into the world.

The Place...The Altar

We have an altar from which those who minister at the tabernacle have no right to eat. (Hebrews 13:10)

The Old Testament altar was a place of communication, covenant, and blood. It was here that men worshiped God on altars of earth, stones, bronze or gold. Noah offered a sacrifice on an altar following the flood.

Abraham received the promises of God at an altar. Ancient altars became the meeting place where God encountered his people.

In the book of Exodus, God instructed Moses to craft two specific altars for the Tabernacle. The first of these altars was a bronze altar, a place where the guilty met with God to find absolution. Located outside the Tabernacle tent, it symbolized Christ and his redemptive work on the cross.

The number five represents grace in the Bible, and this altar reflected grace in all of its dimensions. It measured five by five by five cubits in dimension. The bronze altar had five designated utensils, provided for five different types of offerings, and sacrificed five distinct animals. At this altar, God's grace was poured out upon his people.

The second altar was located inside the tent. The golden altar of incense stood before a curtain which separated the Holy of Holies from the rest of the Tabernacle.

Twice a day, a priest would burn prescribed incense before God's presence. This altar represented Christ as the mediator and intercessor between God and man. It was a place of worship and prayer and pointed to Christ's triumph.

These two Old Testament altars represented a place of divine intervention. Through grace and intercession, the Old Testament priests connected with God through prayer and sacrifice.

In the New Testament, the significance of the altar expands to take new spiritual meaning. When Christ died on the cross, he entered a heavenly tabernacle and placed his blood upon an eternal altar. We access this spiritual altar when we prepare to minister:

> ... *he(Christ) went through the greater and more perfect tabernacle that is not man-made, that is to say, not a part of this creation. He did not enter by means of the blood of goats and calves; but he entered the Most Holy Place once for all by his own blood, having obtained eternal redemption...(Hebrews 9:11-12)*

We no longer stand at a physical altar in the midst of an earthly Tabernacle. Christ's sacrifice on the cross has purchased a new "altar" of unlimited grace for us.

Today, our altar is anywhere ministry occurs.

As we prepare to pray with others, we literally position ourselves at the heavenly altar. Here we find grace to help in times of need.

This is the place of blood, for Christ shed his blood for mankind. It is a place of covenant, for we have an everlasting covenant with God according to his word. It is a place of sacrifice, for Jesus Christ the "Lamb of God" forever satisfied God's requirement for a regular blood sacrifice.

The Provision..The Sacrifices

*Christ loved us and gave himself
up for us as a fragrant offering and
sacrifice to God. (Ephesians 5:1)*

Just as the first altars and early priesthood clarify our purpose and spiritual position at the modern altar, the Old Testament sacrifices also point to a greater New Testament revelation. These offerings represent Christ's work at the altar and the grace which is now available to us.

Sacrifices were a part of daily life for the Old Testament priests. They were integral to the lives and celebrations of Israel. The book of Leviticus describes five basic sacrifices as burnt, grain, fellowship, sin, and the guilt offering. The atoning work of Christ can be seen in each of these offerings.

The Burnt Offering was consumed entirely by fire on the bronze altar (Leviticus 1). It was a free will offering and represented an act of dedication and submission.

In a similar manner, Christ gave himself completely to the altar of the cross. He allowed the will of the Father to become his only purpose:

*...just as Christ loved us and gave
himself up for us as a fragrant offering and
sacrifice to God. (Ephesians 5:2)*

We also present ourselves voluntarily and completely as a burnt offering before God. In light of this understanding, Romans 12:1 takes on new meaning with regards to the burnt offering:

> *Therefore, I urge you, brothers, in view of God's mercy, to offer your bodies as living sacrifices, holy and pleasing to God—this is your spiritual act of worship. (Romans 12:1)*

The Grain Offering was the only one that did not require the shedding of blood. It consisted of the first fruits of the harvest. Grain was baked, fried or cooked in a pan and offered at the bronze altar. Scripture dictated that the offering be mixed with three elements: frankincense, oil, and salt. These elements symbolized prayer and intercession, the Holy Spirit, and the covenant Israel had with God.

The Peace or Fellowship Offering was a joyful celebration of peace, prosperity, and God's provision for Israel. Each Israelite was commanded by God to celebrate and partake of the sacrifice in the presence of the Lord. In this way they recognized God's goodness and provision to their family.

Because of Christ, we can live an abundant life. As we connect or reconcile with others, we share in the goodness of God. As spiritual priests, we minister peace, prosperity, and provision:

Through Jesus, therefore, let us continually
offer to God a sacrifice of praise—the fruit of
lips that confess his name. And do not forget to
do good and to share with others, for with such
sacrifices God is pleased. (Hebrews 13:15-16)

The Sin Offering was required if any Israelite broke a commandment given by the Lord. Only the fat of the animal was burnt on the bronze altar. The rest of the sacrifice was taken outside the camp and burnt on a wood fire at an ash heap.

Christ fulfilled these requirements of the law by becoming the Passover "Lamb of God" that took away the sin of the world. Like the animals that were taken outside the encampment and burned, Christ was crucified outside the walls of Jerusalem. Through his sacrifice, he has purchased our salvation and we are free to share this gift with all mankind:

God made him who had no sin to be sin
for us, so that in him we might become the
righteousness of God. (2 Corinthians 5:21)

The Guilt or Trespass Offering was also a mandatory sacrifice. Its purpose was to restore relationships between people.

The trespass offering covered areas like deception, defilement, concealing the truth, ignorance, violence, unfairness, and keeping things that belong to someone else. It provided a way for a transgression to be eliminated, fellowship restored, and the community of faith to function peacefully.

Again, Christ's sacrifice provided a means for us to be reconciled to God. We are restored to one another and can live life unencumbered by guilt:

When you were dead in your sins and in the uncircumcision of your sinful nature, God made you alive with Christ. He forgave us all our sins, having canceled the written code, with its regulations, that was against us and that stood opposed to us; he took it away, nailing it to the cross. (Colossians 2:12-13)

Because we are forgiven and have experienced God's grace, we can share that with others. Restoration is available at the altar and Christ has paved the way for relationships to be healed and fellowship reinstated.

The altar, the priest, and the sacrifices are the Biblical basis for altar and prayer ministry. Christ was the altar; he serves as the high priest; he became the sacrifices. Through Him, we appropriate the work of grace in our own lives.

When we stand at the altar, either the physical altar of a church or the spiritual altar before his presence, we receive the benefits of what Christ accomplished. We can look to the prophetic example of the Tabernacle as our guide. Jesus satisfied all of the requirements of the Law of Moses. His sacrifice has opened the door to unlimited and unmerited grace towards humanity.

When we begin to minister, we can rest in the fact that our position is sure. The blood of Christ has purchased victory in every area of life. God's provision is available and the anointing is alive and viable to fulfill every need.

Chapter 3
THE ARSENAL OF GOD

One of the many names for God is the *Lord of Hosts* or *Jehovah Sabaoth*. In this designation, the word "hosts" refers to the armies of God, the heavenly powers, and the angels that act at the Lord's command. The root word *saba* means "to wage war." He is a God of warfare.

Prayer ministry is one form of battle that the Lord of Hosts oversees. When we pray, we engage as a soldier of the Lord. In turn, he provides for us and equips us with the necessary armaments to be effective.

Heaven has a full arsenal at our disposal. It contains every weapon to vanquish the enemy and bring salvation, healing, or deliverance to those who are crying out for relief.

What are these divine weapons? How do we access them?

The first step is to understand the artillery he supplies. Then we become familiar with how each is used. Finally, we learn the circumstances where these weapons are appropriate.

Ministry has no formula, but there are some fundamental concepts that make up this weaponry of God. As we continue to stoke our spiritual fire, we are going to examine several spiritual principles which hold the key to our success.

Authority

Have you ever watched a policeman standing in the middle of the road, holding up his hand and directing the flow of traffic? A mere man is no physical match for an oncoming car, much less a truck loaded with merchandise. The policeman stands as a representative of the entire government. He or she has been given jurisdiction and the right to rule in a specific area.

As he directs one lane of traffic to stop and another to go, he acts with the faith that these automobiles will obey his commands and move accordingly. He stands in a place of authority.

"Authority" is simply the right to act. God-given authority positions us in a place of dominion where the power of God can be released. Every believer has been given that gift.

In the beginning, God gave authority to mankind in the Garden of Eden. He gave them dominion over his entire creation. (Genesis 1:27-30) Because mankind was made in his image, God granted him this privilege to act on his behalf.

Adam exercised rule in God's name, but he forfeited this right when he sinned. Christ, the second Adam (1 Corinthians 15:14) reinstated that right of authority with his victory on the cross.

As the second Adam, Christ demonstrated his authority over all of creation. He confirmed his influence over the fish of the sea. (Luke 5:4-6) He calmed the storm (Luke 8:22-25) and walked on water. (Matthew 14:25-27) He showed his authority over sickness and disease and even death itself. (Matthew 4:23-24. Jesus was superior over demonic powers. (Matthew 17:14-18) He had the ability to forgive sins (Luke 5:24) and to judge. (John 5:27) His parting words to his disciples were, *All authority in heaven and on earth has been given to me.* (Matthew 28:18)

The Apostle Paul understood the supreme position of Christ over all of Creation. He described it like this:

...(God) seated him at his right hand in the heavenly realms, far above all rule and authority,

power and dominion, and every title that can be given, not only in the present age but also in the one to come. And God placed all things under his feet and appointed him to be head over everything for the church, which is his body, the fullness of him who fills everything in every way. (Ephesians 1:20-23)

However, it is not enough to merely acknowledge the authority that Jesus commands. We must realize that Jesus transferred that same authority to the disciples. Why? So that they could continue the work of the kingdom:

When Jesus had called the Twelve together, he gave them power and authority to drive out all demons and to cure diseases, and he sent them out to preach the kingdom of God and to heal the sick. (Luke 9:1)

God has positioned believers today alongside his Son in that very same place of power and authority. As his body, we are seated beside him in the heavenly realms:

And God raised us up with Christ and seated us with him in the heavenly realms in Christ Jesus, in order that in the coming ages he might show the incomparable riches of his grace, expressed in his kindness to us in Christ Jesus. (Ephesians 2:6-7)

We are Christ's representatives on this earth. We are ambassadors for his heavenly realm. Therefore, we are equipped to carry out our God-given assignment. Jesus said, *I have given you authority to trample on snakes and scorpions and to overcome all the power of the enemy; nothing will harm you.* (Luke 10:19)

The Name of Jesus

As we begin to activate our faith, we reach out with the grace that Christ has given us. But it is not our strength or position that has power. Authority is found by using the name of Jesus. It is his name that carries weight in the spiritual realm.

During the last week of his life, Jesus bequeathed the right to use his name. His early disciples, as well as modern-day followers of Christ, have permission to act using the name of Jesus. We should trust that he will stand behind his word. As we minister with faith, it is as though Jesus was present doing the work himself:

> *I tell you the truth, anyone who has faith in me will do what I have been doing. He will do even greater things than these, because I am going to the Father. And I will do whatever you ask in my name, so that the Son may bring glory to the Father. You may ask me for anything in my name, and I will do it. (John 14:12-14)*

So we are positioned in the authority of our Lord and Savior Jesus. We pray and minister using his name and at his prompting. We pray for healing "in the name of Jesus." We cast out demons "in the name of Jesus." Anything we ask or do for the Kingdom of God should be done "in the name of Jesus" because he has promised to answer that request.

Therefore, our confidence is not in ourselves, but in Christ. It is his name that wields the power.

The Blood of Christ

What can wash away my sins? Nothing but the blood of Jesus. What can make me whole again? Nothing but the blood of Jesus.

In the last chapter, we discussed the Old Testament sacrifices. The blood of animals covered the sins of the people and nation. The blood reconciled those who were estranged and redeemed a nation to its Creator.

When Jesus died on the cross he offered his own blood as the one final sacrifice. The blood of Christ opened a new covenant of life and made all things possible:

This is my blood of the covenant, which is poured out for many for the forgiveness of sins. (Matthew 26:28)

In him we have redemption through his blood, the forgiveness of sins, in accordance with the riches of God's grace that he lavished on us. (Ephesians 1:7)

The blood of Christ redeems, reconciles, and has power in other ways. It provides protection for us. The blood of the Passover lamb was applied to the doors in ancient Israel so that the angel of death would pass over the household. The blood of our Passover lamb also covers and protects us from evil.

We can pray and ask for the covering of the blood. By doing so, we tap into its supernatural power. We are cleansed, kept safe, and covered with the life-giving attributes.

Laying on of Hands

How do we release the power of God to another? One method used throughout the Old and New Testament is the "laying on of hands."

This anointed touch relays God's power and grace from one person to another. The action either transfers the power of God to a person or imparts a calling or gift to individuals. Let's take a look at how God used laying on hands in the Bible.

Transference. In the Old Testament men laid their hands upon the offering at the altar and transferred their transgressions to the animal being sacrificed. Aaron and his sons did this as part of their consecration before God. (Exodus 29:10,15,19)

The high priest would also represent the nation of

Israel once a year during the Day of Atonement. He would place his hands upon a goat and impart Israel's iniquity to the goat. Sin was transferred from the guilty nation to an innocent animal. Then the goat was released into the wilderness. This is where we get the phrase "scapegoat."

> *And Aaron shall lay both his hands upon the head of the live goat, and confess over him all the iniquities of the children of Israel, and all their transgressions in all their sins, putting them upon the head of the goat, and shall send him away by the hand of a fit man into the wilderness; and the goat shall bear upon him all their iniquities into a land not inhabited. (Leviticus 16:21-22)*

So, sin is transferred from one to another by the laying on of hands. In the New Testament we are cautioned to be careful when laying hands on someone. This is especially true when dealing with deliverance prayer:

> *Do not be hasty in the laying on of hands, and do not share in the sins of others. Keep yourself pure. 1 Timothy 5:22*

Impartation. The laying on of hands also became part of spiritual ceremonies and ministry. It accompanied the recognition of new leaders, spiritual acts, healings, blessing, and miracles. God's call to minister was also transferred by the laying on of hands:

• Before Moses died, God commanded him to anoint Joshua to lead the nation of Israel…*Then he (Moses) laid his hands on him (Joshua) and commissioned him, as the LORD instructed through Moses.* (Numbers 27:23)

• In Acts 13:3, the apostles released Paul and Barnabas for the work of the ministry through this method... *So after they had fasted and prayed, they placed their hands on them and sent them off.*

• Jesus also put his hands on the children to pray for them and bless them. He also ministered healing by laying his hands on the masses:.. *He could not do any miracles there, except lay his hands on a few sick people and heal them.* (Mark 6:5);

Once more Jesus put his hands on the man's eyes. Then his eyes were opened, his sight was restored, and he saw everything clearly. (Mark 8:25)

Then he put his hands on her, and immediately she straightened up and praised God. (Luke 13:3)

• The baptism of the Holy Spirit was also characterized by the disciples laying hands on new believers...*Then Peter and John placed their hands on them, and they received the Holy Spirit.* (Acts 8:17)

• Miracles were also done by the hands of the apostles. (Acts 19:11)

• The gifts of the Holy Spirit were given as a result of laying on of hands, as in the case of Timothy: *Do not neglect your gift, which was given you through prophecy when the body of elders laid their hands on you.* (1 Timothy 4:14)

As ministers of God, we transfer and impart the grace and power of our Savior. By simply touching an individual, we connect them to a power source that is able to meet their every need. Placing our hands upon them initiates this process and helps us to release the presence of God within us.

Anointing Oil

Specialized oil called "anointing oil" was used throughout the Old Testament. In the tabernacle, this anointing oil required a specific formula known only to the priests. Quite often, it was used in conjunction with the laying on of hands. This fragrant liquid represented the presence and approval of God.

Men anointed objects and people that were set aside for sacred use. The elements of the tabernacle were anointed with oil. Kings, prophets, and priests entered into service after having oil poured upon them.

In the New Testament, we see that Jesus Christ was known as the Messiah or "anointed one." The term signified God's power and presence resting upon his life.

The descent of the Holy Spirit at Jesus baptism is further proof of the connection between anointing, power, and service. He indicated that this anointing set him apart and qualified him to proclaim the good news to Israel:

> *The Spirit of the Lord is on me, because*
> *he has anointed me to proclaim good*
> *news to the poor. (Luke 4:18)*

As his children, we also carry the anointing of the Holy Spirit upon us:

> *Now it is God who makes both us and you*
> *stand firm in Christ. He anointed us, set his*
> *seal of ownership on us, and put his Spirit in*
> *our hearts as a deposit, guaranteeing what*
> *is to come. (2 Corinthians 1:21-22)*

For ministry purposes, anointing oil symbolizes the power of the Holy Spirit. It is used in healing ministry. It also affirms and releases new leadership roles within the kingdom of God.

James advises anointing the sick for healing:

Is anyone among you sick? Let them call the elders of the church to pray over them and <u>anoint them with oil </u>in the name of the Lord. And the prayer offered in faith will make the sick person well; the Lord will raise them up. If they have sinned, they will be forgiven. (James 5:14-15)

Anointing with oil was also a part of the apostles' healing ministry:

They went out and preached that people should repent. They drove out many demons and <u>anointed many sick people with oil </u>and healed them. (Mark 6:12–13)

Today, anointing oils are readily available through retail outlets, bookstores, and online sources. They come in a variety of fragrances depending on the herbs and spices used to compose them. Pure olive oil is also a common choice. Keep in mind, it is not the oil itself, but the oil in conjunction with faith and prayer that makes the difference.

Giving and Receiving

Jesus told his twelve disciples before sending them out,"…*freely ye have received, freely give.*"(Matthew 10:8) What did he mean by those words? What was it they had received that Jesus wanted imparted to others?

When we encounter Christ, we are filled with his Spirit. The Holy Spirit dwells within us and is able to move through us to others in need. But we need to be continually filled. That is the essence of the scripture from Ephesians 5:18 that says *be filled with the Spirit*. It is a never-ending filling up. One time is not enough.

To give out of our spiritual resources, we must first learn to receive the grace and power of God on a personal level. How we receive depends upon the individual. Some encounter God in prayer. Others during worship. And still many prefer the reading and study of God's word to feed and fill their spirit. Once filled, then we release it to others.

The anointing and power of God flow like a river during ministry. We must understand how to cooperate with the anointing and not be moving cross current to it. Like water in a garden hose, the flow is either going out of the hose or coming into it.

In ministry situations, it is our responsibility to focus on giving to others. That is the reason we are there. Their part is to receive.

Giving to God. When we release our worship and praise to him, we are in the giving mode. We take what is in us and impart that to God. We sing, praise, pray, read his word and bless him out of our spirit.

However, when we are is in this condition, the flow is

outward from us and directed to God. To receive from the Lord, we need to switch over to the receiving mode. This requires focusing on receiving, not on giving.

Receiving from God. I believe one of the greatest obstacles to effective ministry is the inability of people to receive directly from God. His power is present when we pray, but we do not always understand how to connect with it.

When I minister, I instruct the person to just soak up the anointing of the Lord like a sponge. A sponge is dry, but very absorbent and has the ability to absorb large quantities of water. Note that the sponge is not squeezing out any of its liquid, but just taking it in at this time.

We have the capacity to absorb the power of the Holy Spirit when it is present. This is receiving.

Problems occur when someone is waiting for God to move and yet attempting to worship him at the same time. They are usually so focused on adoration that they forget to take in what is already present. They need to switch to a receiving mode instead.

We don't need to prove our love to move the hand of God. All of God's blessings are reflections of his grace. There is nothing we can do or say that would be sufficient or even begin to qualify us. Jesus Christ has already performed that work. We approach God believing he is ready and able to supply all of our need.

Then we need to merely receive it. In an "attitude" of worship, we accept the grace he bestows upon us.

As we prepare to minister to others, we can adopt this same posture. Receive from him and allow him to saturate your inner man before you begin to pray for others. Be filled with the Spirit!

Focus on receiving and then releasing God's goodness to others. No one wants to end up like the Dead Sea in Israel. It only receives from the Jordan River and has no outlet. There is no flow, no life, and the water becomes stagnant.

When we have been filled by God, then we are in a position to release his power. We receive ourselves and then give to others.

The Armor of God

Our final weapon in the arsenal of God is his armor. Paul wrote to the Ephesian church concerning the armor of God. He had lived several years chained to a Roman guard so Paul knew firsthand the importance of each piece of armament. The Romans were experts in warfare.

In the last chapter of Ephesians, Paul writes:

Finally, be strong in the Lord and in his mighty power. Put on the full armor of God, so that you can take your stand against the devil's schemes...

Stand firm then, with the belt of truth buckled around your waist, with the breastplate of righteousness in place, and with your feet fitted with the readiness that comes from the gospel of peace. In addition to all this, take up the shield of faith, with which you can extinguish all the flaming arrows of the evil one. Take the helmet of salvation and the sword of the Spirit, which is the word of God. (Ephesians 6:17)

When we enter into spiritual battle, we have both offensive and defensive weapons. On the offense, God gives us the power to use his word as a mighty sword to defeat the enemy. We wield it skillfully in prayer and proclamation over those who receive prayer.

Defensively, we are reminded to put on truth, righteousness,and the life-giving message of the gospel. Most importantly, we lift the shield of faith against the onslaught of our enemy. The battle is not one-sided...we will face opposition. Our protection comes from remembering all aspects of the armor and dressing for spiritual battle accordingly.

God trains us for success in ministry. As we utilize the various armaments from his arsenal, we are thoroughly prepared to be effective minsters.

Chapter 4
SPIRITUAL GIFTS

When God calls us to minister, he equips us for the job. In the last chapter we talked about the arsenal of God and the many weapons he gives us. Now, let's take a look at how the Holy Spirit directs us to use them.

Communication with God is critical during ministry times. As the Holy Spirit partners with us in the process, learning to hear his direction is of vital importance. Our ability to cooperate with the Holy Spirit begins with the ability to hear his voice.

Hearing the Voice of God

Each of us has a spiritual radar, a God sensing device that is attuned to the spiritual realm. God's word tells us that his sheep hear his voice. If you are one of his children, then you do hear his voice!

However, each one of us has a different way to hear. Some of us hear a quiet, still voice in our inner man. Others see pictures or have visions as God speaks to them. These supernatural revelations require interpretation and understanding that come through experience and maturation.

Many have strong impressions of what we are supposed to do. Certain actions or words seem right, but there is no explanation as to how you know…you just know!

Quite often, God uses his word to speak to us. Scriptures that we know or are familiar with bubble forth out of us as God directs us in times of ministry.

In all of these varied ways, God is speaking to us and directing our actions.

How do we know that we are seeing, hearing, and sensing God or just imagining things in our own minds?

We know that it is God speaking to us by **the way he comes to us.** He doesn't come with force trying to wrestle us into doing something. Instead, he comes to us gently with a quiet nudge, an impression, or a picture of what he wants us to do.

We also know that it's God speaking to us by **the relevance of what he says.** Does it apply and meet the needs of the person?

Finally, we know that it's God causing us to move in one of his charismatic gifts by **the fruit that it produces.** God brings conviction not condemnation.

The Holy Spirit is the spirit of truth, and he comes with a merciful presence. His goal is to make us whole. He heals us and helps us walk in our created destiny. God doesn't come to make us feel guilty, condemned, or hopeless. After each time encounter, the person receiving ministry should walk away feeling uplifted, enlightened, and full of hope.

This is the purpose of the spiritual gifts. God wants to move in us and through us to bless others. And he's looking for those who will listen, act in faith, and be a partner with him. God desires to touch the lives of people and their needs.

Gifts of Grace

You are blessed with spiritual gifts. They are not earned in any way, but offered because of his great love and compassion for people. They are gifts of grace freely given by a generous God to equip his people for service.

All of God's gifts are good. James 1:17 tells us that *every good and perfect gift is from above, coming down from the father of the heavenly lights, who does not change like shifting shadows.* He is the giver of good and perfect gifts!

God asks us to be stewards of these gifts, especially during times of ministry. These spiritual tools within every believer serve a singular purpose…to help one another. The apostle Peter wrote to his disciples:

> *…each one should use whatever gift he has received to serve others, faithfully administering God's grace in its various forms. So that in all things God may be praised through Jesus Christ. To him be the glory and the power for ever and ever. (1 Peter 4:10 – 11)*

As we begin to look at the many spiritual gifts that are available, we should first realize that it is a spirit of wisdom and revelation that is operating in our lives. Ephesians Chapter 1 says this:

> *I keep asking that the God of our Lord Jesus Christ, the glorious father, may give you the spirit of wisdom and revelation, so that you may know him better. (Ephesians 1:17)*

When we receive revelation from God, it is like seeing into a hidden spiritual realm. Revelation is the easy part. The more challenging assignment is maturing with wisdom so that we may interpret, communicate, and apply the revelation.

Now, let's examine these marvelous revelatory gifts. God desires for us to understand and use them as we cooperate with him in times of ministry.

The Charismatic Gifts

(The following is a basic description of the charismatic spiritual gifts
and their use. For a more detailed study, refer to my coming book
Equipped.)

*Now about spiritual gifts, brothers, I do not want
you to be ignorant...There are different kinds of
gifts, but the same Spirit. There are different kinds
of service, but the same Lord. There are different
kinds of working, but the same God works all of
them in all men. (1 Corinthians 12:1, 4-6)*

The Apostle Paul wrote to the Corinthian church
about the use of spiritual gifts. He began with these
words: *I do not want you to be ignorant.* What did
Paul mean?

The Apostle Paul was concerned about their
understanding and use of the these expressions. The
Corinthian church was active in ministry. They were
operating in these spiritual gifts, but the results were
chaotic!

In an effort to bring some order to their services,
Paul wrote to the church and addressed the problem
in 1 Corinthians Chapters 12-14. He didn't want the
church to be ignorant about what they were doing
and why they were doing it.

Paul told the Corinthian church three basic facts about
the charismatic gifts. First, Paul wrote that there are

different kinds of gifts, but the same Spirit. Although there are different kinds and expressions of gifts, it is the Holy Spirit activating our spiritual individuality. The Holy Spirit touches these divine deposits bringing them to life.

Second, there are different kinds of service, but the same Lord. Paul is referring to how the nine gifts operate. The Holy Spirit is the root, but there are many branches of service and each is distinctive. Some are verbal, others are demonstrative, and still others more revelatory.

Finally, Paul states that there are different kinds of working, but the same God works all of them in all men. Each of us has different gifts, even a combination of different gifts, but how they work through us can look very different from one person to another. The outward appearance is unique to every believer.

God chooses to use these special manifestations of his nature for several purposes. Sometimes they proclaim the gospel message and awaken people to the existence of a loving God. The gifts also build the kingdom of God. They are meant to glorify God and the demonstration of his power. Spiritual gifts also help us to identify who we are and who others are in the body of Christ.

We will discover that the gifts are dependent and yet interdependent upon one another. That's the way

God created them. And most importantly, they are energized by love. Throughout Chapters 12-14 Paul encourages the Corinthian church to be in unity. He warns the church in 1 Corinthians 13:1-3 that these gifts are secondary to the greatest treasure of God… his love.

The Apostle Paul did not want believers to be ignorant. God expects us to minister out of a heart of compassion, mercy, and his love which flows through us. What he asks from us is to trust him, believe him, and minister in faith. We are merely the channels of love and blessing as we become his mouth, his hands, and his voice.

The Voice of God

But the manifestation of the Spirit is given to each one for the profit of all: for to one is given the word of wisdom through the Spirit, to another the word of knowledge through the same Spirit, to another faith by the same Spirit, to another gifts of healings by the same Spirit, to another the working of miracles, to another prophecy, to another discerning of spirits, to another different kinds of tongues, to another the interpretation of tongues. (1 Corinthians 12:7-10 NKJV)

The nine different charismatic gifts can be subdivided into three classifications: the Voice of

God, the Hand of God, and the Mind of God. They are listed separately in 1 Corinthians 12 and we will examine them individually. These manifestations of God's power frequently flow in combination with one another. We will start with the verbal gifts and the Voice of God which bring inspiration to the hearer.

Prophecy is speaking a message from God in a known language to strengthen, encourage, and comfort others.

It begins with a sense of the Holy Spirit drawing or leading in that direction. Sometimes it may feel like a physical bubbling forth, almost like a fountain within our spirit. Occasionally, one hears the words that the Holy Spirit speaks. Often, it may be the first few words that prompt us to begin and then the Holy Spirit completes the message as we speak. Many people have visions or see pictures that they begin to put into words.

As we attune to the Holy Spirit, our spiritual antennas receive the messages of God. Prophecy is a verbal release of that gift.

Different Kinds of Tongues and Interpretation of Tongues. These two gifts work hand in hand. What is Tongues? It is an earthly or celestial language that is not learned, but spoken by believers as the Holy Spirit gives them utterance. It may be in a known earthly language, but can be foreign or of a heavenly origin.

We should distinguish between corporate Tongues as a gift and private tongues as a personal prayer language.

Everyone may speak in tongues and strengthen their spirit with a personal prayer language. But the gift that we refer to here is the charismatic gift of tongues. It is a public corporate message in tongues given specifically to another person or a group of people.

The Interpretation of Tongues translates the message into a known language. As the Holy Spirit releases the meaning, just like prophecy, the words are spoken to a public gathering.

Tongues and Interpretation of Tongues is equivalent to prophecy. It is a two-part message that is unknown and then becomes revealed as the interpretation is spoken. Usually, the interpretation is given right after the message in tongues. When speaking a message in tongues, either you or someone on your team may have the interpretation.

The Hand of God

The next three gifts are Faith, Working of Miracles, and Gifts of Healings. These three gifts are characterized as the Hand of God. They represent a demonstration of his divine power.

Faith comes in many forms. Each of us has a measure of faith (Romans 12:3), there is a saving faith (Ephesians 2:10), and faith is also a fruit of the spirit (Galatians 5:22).

However, the charismatic gift of Faith is something more than that. This Faith is a supernatural deposit of God that goes beyond our proportion of faith. It is a divinely inspired belief which casts out all doubt and has complete belief and trust in God. There is no wavering, no questioning, but only complete trust that God is able willing and will do what he said he would.

Charismatic Faith is also a catalyst that may trigger the other gifts of God. It does not stand alone, but moves in conjunction with the other gifts like healing. It's a bulldog-kind of faith that simply won't let go. This gift of faith can be imparted through dreams and visions, an inspired word of teaching, a word spoken by God, or even reading the Bible.

Working of Miracles is a display of God's power that interrupts the natural flow of the physical laws of the universe. Jesus fed five thousand with five loaves of bread and two fish. Paul raised a dead man to life after he fell from a window.

Miracles are generally instantaneous as opposed to healings which may occur over a period of time.

The Working of Miracles is a sign. It is a visual demonstration of power showing evidence of a creator and his kingdom. The activity of power awes and amazes those who witness it. Miracles demonstrate God's attributes of love, justice, and even judgment. They reveal his glory.

When people are raised from the dead, water turns to wine, or someone evangelizes and thousands come to the Lord, it is a miracle of God. The Apostle Paul wrote this in 1 Corinthians 2:4–5:

My message and my preaching were not with wise and persuasive words but with a demonstration of the Spirit's power so that your faith may not rest on men's wisdom but on God's power.

The Gifts of Healings refer to the supernatural manifestation of the Holy Spirit that heals outside of natural cures. Jesus healed the blind, the lame, and all that were brought to him with physical afflictions. Peter healed the cripple at the Gate Beautiful.

Healing is not always immediate. Even when Jesus prayed, the lepers in Luke 17:14 were healed as they went on their way. Often the gifts of healings involves word of wisdom or word of knowledge. Faith activates this gift. (more in the Healing section of the book)

Mind of God

The three gifts which characterize the Mind of God are the Word of Knowledge, the Word of Wisdom, and the Discerning of Spirits. These three gifts uncover hidden truths from the spiritual realm and reveal them in the here and now.

The Word of Knowledge is a supernatural impartation of facts from the infinite knowledge of an all-knowing God. These facts can be about a person, place, or event in the past or present. The word of knowledge restores confidence and belief in God and is a tool for evangelism.

Jesus knew all about the Samaritan woman when he said *the man you now have is not your husband* (John 4:18). Peter understood that Ananias and Sophia were lying in Acts Chapter 5.

God communicates the Word of Knowledge in various ways. It can take the form of simply knowing or a strong impression. It can also come as a dream or vision. Many people see words associated with others or highlighted body parts.

In combination with the gifts of healings, the Word of Knowledge can feel like one of your body parts aches or is in pain. For some, it is hearing God's voice as he speaks a revelation. The word may appear as letters or words above someone's head. These are just some of the ways that the Word of Knowledge can operate. As stated before, everyone is unique. These gifts work in specialized ways through different individuals.

The Word of Wisdom is a supernatural insight into God's will and purposes. It reveals direction or plans of action.

Peter was given a Word of Wisdom when he had the

vision on the rooftop: *Get up, Peter. Kill and eat.* (Acts 10:13) It was a godly command for Peter to take the gospel to a Gentile named Cornelius.

The Holy Spirit communicates the Word of Wisdom similarly to the Word of Knowledge. It can also come as scriptural insight from the word of God. Occasionally, the Holy Spirit may surprise you as you find yourself speaking words that are unprepared and spontaneous.

The Discerning of Spirits is our final charismatic gift. It is the supernatural gift which enables believers to distinguish or perceive influences, spirits, and anointings. The Apostle Paul perceived that a fortune teller was under the influence of an evil spirit and commanded it to come out of her in Acts 16:18.

Often people think that Discerning of Spirits is recognizing demons behind every corner. That is only a small part of the operation of this gift. The Discerning of Spirits identifies an angelic presence as well as an evil presence.

God communicates this gift through our spiritual senses. Like our physical senses, we may note a resemblance to another person that we know. God is connecting the dots and showing us that there is a similarity between the two people.

He may identify a spirit with words which we hear in our inner man. Discerning of Spirits may come through touch as we lay hands on a person. It can also come through taste and smell as some people sense supernatural influences in their surroundings, sicknesses, or other conditions on people that they ministered to. A foul smell or bitter taste indicates the presence of an evil spirit. A sweet-smelling odor reveals the presence of Jesus.

Many people who operate in this gift pick up on the emotions of others. They feel similar sentiments or spiritual influences that are affecting that person.

Finally, the Discerning of Spirits is also used in identifying and confirming gifts and callings. It helps to distinguish between false and true brethren.

God designed these nine charismatic spiritual gifts to equip believers for service. Whether in the church, the marketplace, or out in the community, God is ready to make himself known. He is looking for vessels that will carry his gifts to a hurting humanity.

Chapter 5

SALVATION: A GIFT OF GRACE

Salvation is a one-size-fits-all gift from God. It is available to young and old, male and female, across every cultural border throughout the world.

With his sacrifice on the cross, Christ provided a means for all of us to experience the grace and mercy of our God. He opened a door for wayward people to return and have a relationship with their heavenly Father.

Eternal reward and everlasting life await anyone who accepts Christ as Saviour. This is the basic premise of salvation; however, God designed it to affect a greater realm than just heaven.

Both the Old and New Testament reflect this wider understanding of God's provision. By examining the Biblical meaning of salvation presented in both Testaments, we can embrace a much larger understanding of what it means to be "saved."

The Old Testament concept of salvation contained three parts. First, it implied that there was a person or nation in deep distress. In other words, something or someone needed help. In the Book of Judges, the Philistines oppressed and afflicted Israel.

Second, it involved a deliverer. Someone acted on the behalf of the sufferer in order to rescue them from their distress. Using the Book of Judges as an example, we read about a deliverer being chosen and empowered by God's hand.

Third, the deliverer released the afflicted party from the circumstances that caused the suffering. Deborah, Gideon, Samson and others defeated the enemies of Israel in Judges. So, salvation displayed movement from distress to safety by the power of someone greater.

Other types of Old Testament salvation can be seen through the lives of significant men in ancient times. Joseph, the son of Patriarch Israel, "saved" his family from famine when he became second in command to Pharaoh of Egypt. Moses delivered the nation of Israel from the hands of Pharaoh.

In the New Testament, "salvation" reflects many similarities to the Old Testament concept. The Greek word *sozo*, "to save," implies rescue from life-threatening danger. It occurs over one hundred times in the New Testament.

In some contexts *sozo* refers to deliverance from physical threat (Acts 27:30) or in saving one's life . (John 12:27) At other times the word *sozo* is related to Jesus' miracles of healing and means "to restore to health and wholeness." The word describes God's manifold action through Christ to deliver humanity from the life-draining powers of sin, death, and demonic oppression.

Salvation is designed to establish joy and impart the security of eternal relationship with God. With this in mind, we can interpret salvation as affecting the physical state, the soul (mind, will, and emotions), as well as the spiritual condition of man.

Prayer for Salvation

In his letter to the Roman church, the Apostle Paul wrote these instructions about salvation:

> *... If you confess with your mouth, "Jesus is Lord," and believe in your heart that God raised him from the dead, you will be saved. For it is with your heart that you believe and are justified, and it is with your mouth that you confess and are saved. Romans (10:9-10)*

According to this scripture, salvation can be described as a two-step process—confessing and believing. When anyone accepts Christ as the Son of God, believes that Jesus died on the cross for their personal sin, and acknowledges in their heart that Jesus provides new life, they are born again.

This is salvation—old things pass away, and all things become new to the believer. The darkness of sin which cloaked the old life is exchanged for a spotless robe of righteousness. The old life is over; the new life in Christ has begun.

The other important aspect of salvation is an open declaration of belief in Christ. This reaffirms the reality of this spiritual transformation. A change occurs not only in someone's own heart and soul, but also in the realm of the spirit. These words help to solidify the change of heart that has taken place. A verbal confession identifies the new believer as a brother or sister in the Lord.

These two steps, believing and confessing, define the salvation act for the new believer. They are guiding principles to remember when praying with someone for salvation.

Guidelines for Prayer

Other than the scripture from Romans 10, the Bible does not provide any examples of praying for salvation.

Always allow the Holy Spirit to direct your conversation and prayer. He knows and understands the mindset and background of every person.

Some may have grown up in the church and are looking to recommit their lives to Christ. Others may lack any kind of spiritual background. They sense the Holy Spirit drawing them and are responding to his invitation.

It is best to be prepared to answer any of these questions. The following points are some of the common areas of misunderstanding that people frequently have.

Explain salvation. Some people do not understand what salvation is or what it does. Be prepared to clarify the basic doctrine of salvation to the person you are praying with. This doesn't need to take long. Just a few brief statements to explain the spiritual transaction.

I usually share that we pray in faith believing that Jesus died for our wrongdoings. Be careful about using Christian terms to describe salvation. The person may not understand what you mean.

I also emphasize the fact that God forgives us when we ask. And I include some thoughts about how we are new creatures with a bright future. Their past is forgotten in God's eyes.

Jesus is God's only son. There are religions that teach God has many sons and each of us can become a god. Others believe that Jesus might be one in a long list of "gods" who they recognize and serve.

You may need to distinguish Christianity from these other belief systems.

> *The Word became flesh and made his dwelling among us. We have seen his glory, the glory of the <u>One and Only</u>, who came from the Father, full of grace and truth. (John 1:14)*

Jesus is the only way to the Father. Many today acknowledge a choice of pathways to godliness and eternal life. They believe each religion has its own acceptable way to relate to God. But Jesus told the crowd in Jerusalem, *"I am the way, the truth, and the life. No one comes to the Father except through me."*(John 14:6)

Jesus died for the sins of everyone. Christ died for each of our individual sins, as well as the sins that plague our fallen world. From a toddling child to the aged man lying on his deathbed, everyone is within reach of our Savior Jesus Christ. Even the thief who hung on a cross beside Jesus found saving grace in his eyes. (Luke 23:43)

> *For God so loved the world that he gave his one and only Son, that whoever believes in him shall not perish but have eternal life. For God did not send his Son into the world to condemn the world, but to save the world through him. (John 3:15-17)*

The blood of Jesus cleanses us from all sin. Every sin

can be forgiven. Every vile act can be cleansed by the blood of Christ. He has provided a new life and fresh start for each of us.

In January 1989, Ted Bundy, a convicted serial rapist and killer, was electrocuted in Florida. He had been linked to at least twenty-three murders of young women, but in reality there were probably more. In the final days of his life, he accepted the forgiveness of Jesus Christ and became a Christian. James Dobson of Focus on the Family witnessed Bundy's remorse over his heinous crimes and could testify to the killer's change of heart. Bundy died as a "sinner saved by grace." Indeed, no one is exempt from the saving love of Christ.

In him we have redemption through his blood, the forgiveness of sins, in accordance with the riches of God's grace. Ephesians 1:7

You will become a new creation. The eternal life that Jesus provides destroys the old man and his patterns of behavior. It supplies the power to overcome our shortcomings. Bad habits fall away. Everything is fresh and clean in the life of a new believer.

The old nature that wanted to please only itself and its evil desires is replaced by a new longing to know God and His ways. The curse of sin is broken and the blessing of knowing God begins.

> *Therefore, if anyone is in Christ, he is*
> *a new creation; the old has gone, the new*
> *has come! (2 Corinthians 5:17)*

You cannot earn salvation. No one can earn God's salvation; it is a gift. There is nothing that qualifies us for this gift and nothing that disqualifies us from receiving it. Money, good deeds, or moral sacrifice will never earn salvation. It is God's delight to simply give us his kingdom.

Not everyone understands this concept of "free" grace. My friend Carla thought she needed to earn a position with Christ. She assured me that one day she would attend church, but first she needed to get herself together. My friend equated church attendance with salvation, a common mistake!

Jesus does not demand that we get clean before we come to him—that is what salvation is all about. Cleansing is his job!

> *For it is by grace you have been saved,*
> *through faith—and this not from yourselves,*
> *it is the gift of God— not by works, so that*
> *no one can boast. Ephesians 2: 8-9*

Pray for salvation. If you have the honor of leading someone in this prayer, initiate the prayer and ask the person to repeat the words after you. Request that they speak out loud if the situation allows. Try to pray in short word sequences so that they can easily understand and follow your lead. The following is one model of a typical prayer for salvation:

Dear Heavenly Father,

I believe in my heart that Jesus is your Son.

I believe he died on the cross for my sins.

Please forgive me for my mistakes, my failings, and anything that has displeased you.

I confess that Jesus is my Lord and Saviour from this day forth.

I receive new life in Christ.

Thank you for salvation, God. Amen.

Pray for the new believer. After praying with the person, I suggest you now pray for him or her. You might ask if there is any personal area or situation that needs God's intervention.

In your prayer, remember to thank God for his or her decision to accept Christ as personal Savior. Thank God for their new life in Christ. You may also pray a blessing upon the new believer as the Holy Spirit leads. The priestly prayer spoken over the people of Israel is an example:

The LORD bless you and keep you; the LORD make his face shine upon you and be

gracious to you; the LORD turn his face toward
you and give you peace. (Numbers 6:24-26)

Assurance of salvation. After the prayer, I encourage you to review with the person what has just happened. Let them relay in their own words their new relationship with God. This will assure you, as well as them, that something did indeed transpire. Answer any questions that may arise.

Follow up. Congratulate them on their new spiritual birth and encourage them to follow God. You may suggest attending a local church, a small group meeting, or appropriate outreach that teaches the word of God. The new believer is a baby, and just like a natural human baby, he or she will need care and support. God may ask you to be a part of the spiritual growth process.

Salvation is the first step to a renewed and vibrant life in Christ. Rejoice with God for what he has done and thank him for allowing you to participate in the process. Salvation is the most important decision anyone can make.

Chapter 6

BAPTISM OF THE HOLY SPIRIT: THE PROMISE OF POWER

As Jesus was about to leave his disciples and ascend into heaven, he gave them some very specific instructions. He told them to go and make disciples. and then commissioned them to bring the good news to every nation.

In order to accomplish this daunting task, Jesus promised that they would receive power. He gave them instructions to wait for the gift which would equip them for their future ministry:

I am going to send you what my Father has promised; but stay in the city until you have been clothed with power from on high. (Luke 24:49)

In the Book of Acts, Jesus also told his disciples:

> *For John baptized with water, but in a few days you will be baptized with the Holy Spirit. (Acts 1:5)*

Their response to his words was to stay in Jerusalem. As the disciples continued to pray in earnest in the Upper Room, they waited for the promise of their Master.

When the day of Pentecost arrived, the one hundred and twenty men and women encountered the Holy Spirit in a unique way. As the Book of Acts states, the Holy Spirit came as a *rushing mighty wind* and rested upon each of them:

> *And they were all filled with the Holy Ghost,*
> *and began to speak with other tongues, as the*
> *Spirit gave them utterance. (Acts 2:2-4)*

Peter, the disciple who cowered and denied Jesus on the night of his trial, was transformed into a dynamic evangelist. That same day he preached the good news to thousands in Jerusalem!

The coming of the Holy Spirit marked each disciple with the ability to obey Christ's commands to proclaim the gospel. The Holy Spirit ushered in a new era of power.

This event which the one hundred and twenty men and women experienced in Jerusalem is often referred to as the Baptism of the Holy Spirit. It was recorded in the beginning of the Book of Acts, but is readily seen throughout the entire book.

On every occasion, whenever believers came into contact with the Holy Spirit, they received the fullness of that blessing. Note the following instances:

• Peter and John were sent to Samaria because they heard that Samaria had accepted the gospel message. Even though the people had believed in Christ, the Baptism of the Holy Spirit was considered a separate experience. Peter and John ministered this to the Samaritans by laying hands on them and praying.

When they arrived, they prayed for them that they might receive the Holy Spirit, because the Holy Spirit had not yet come upon any of them; they had simply been baptized into the name of the Lord Jesus. Then Peter and John placed their hands on them, and they received the Holy Spirit. (Acts 8:15-17)

• In the house of a God-fearing Roman named Cornelius, the Apostle Peter explained the gospel message. As Cornelius and his household heard Peter's words, the Holy Spirit fell upon them just like at Pentecost—Cornelius, a Gentile, spoke with tongues! Afterwards, the new believers were baptized in water, a separate occurrence differentiating it from the Baptism of the Holy Spirit:

While Peter was still speaking these words, the Holy Spirit came on all who heard the message. The circumcised believers who had come with Peter were astonished that the gift of the Holy Spirit had been poured out even on the Gentiles. For they heard them speaking in tongues and praising God. Then Peter said, "Can anyone keep these people from being baptized with water?" (Acts 10:44-46)

• The Apostle Paul traveled to Ephesus and encountered several new believers. When he asked whether they had received the Holy Spirit, he found they were only familiar with John's baptism for the repentance of sin. When Paul placed his hands on them, they received the Baptism of the Holy Spirit and spoke in tongues.

... (Paul) asked them, "Did you receive the Holy Spirit when you believed?"

They answered, "No, we have not even heard that there is a Holy Spirit."

So Paul asked, "Then what baptism did you receive?"

"John's baptism," they replied.

Paul said, "John's baptism was a baptism of repentance. He told the people to believe in the one coming after him, that is, in Jesus." On hearing this, they were baptized into the name of the Lord Jesus. When Paul placed his hands on them, the Holy Spirit came on them, and they spoke in tongues and prophesied. (Acts 19:2-6)

Understanding the Baptism of the Holy Spirit

So, what exactly is the Baptism of the Holy Spirit and how is this different from salvation?

The Baptism of the Holy Spirit can be explained in this way. All believers in Christ have the Holy Spirit residing in them. When salvation occurs, the Holy Spirit enters a person's life and takes up residence deep within.

I like to compare this to a pool of water. The spiritual pool within a person reflects the glory of God. It mirrors his image just like a body of water reflects and glistens under the radiance of the sun.

But, the Baptism of the Holy Spirit is different. Jesus told his disciples;

> *Whoever believes in me, as the Scripture has said, streams of living water will flow from within him. (John 7:38)*

The Baptism of the Holy Spirit is the release of this spiritual pool into a river of living water. Like a river, the Baptism becomes a powerful force of transformation. It affects both the inner man and outer circumstances. The Holy Spirit flows into a believer's surroundings.

The main evidence that this has occurred is the expression of a new spiritual language, what the Bible calls "tongues."In order to understand this phenomena more completely, let's examine four distinct characteristics about the Baptism of the Holy Spirit.

1. The Baptism of the Holy Spirit is a gift of God's grace. Just like salvation, the Holy Spirit is a gift. And like any gift, you only need to receive, unwrap, and enjoy it!

> *...you shall receive the gift of the*
> *Holy Ghost. (Acts 2:38)*

2. Jesus is the baptizer. The gift of the Holy Spirit comes directly from Jesus. He is the one who does the baptizing.

> *"... he (Jesus) shall baptize you with the*
> *Holy ghost and with fire."(Matthew3:11)*

3. We are commanded to receive. Jesus commanded his disciples to receive the equipping that they would need before they began their ministry. (Acts 1:4) Paul also wrote to fellow believers...*be filled with the Spirit.* (Ephesians 5:18)

4. The gift is for all believers. The Baptism of the Holy Spirit is available to every believer! Jesus did not make a distinction or classify his followers into separate categories.

For the promise is unto you, and to your children, and to all that are afar off, even as many as the Lord our God shall call...(Acts 2:38-40)

The Purpose for the Baptism of the Holy Spirit.

Why is the Baptism of the Holy Spirit so important? What does it mean to the Christian? The following scriptures describe some of the benefits of the Baptism of the Holy Spirit and the advantages of speaking in tongues:

The Baptism of the Holy Spirit enables the believer to be a dynamic witness of the gospel. Remember Peter on the day of Pentecost. He became a powerful witness of Christ to thousands of visiting Jews:

But you will receive power when the Holy Spirit comes on you; and you will be my witnesses in Jerusalem, and in all Judea and Samaria, and to the ends of the earth. Acts 1:8

The Baptism of the Holy Spirit edifies, builds up, and strengthens the believer's spirit. The Baptism of the Holy Spirit helps us maintain a level of spiritual strength. When we pray in tongues, our spirit is energized by God's Spirit and we fortify our inner man:

> *He who speaks in a tongue edifies*
> *himself...(1 Corinthians 14:4)*

> *But you, dear friends, build yourselves*
> *up in your most holy faith and pray*
> *in the Holy Spirit. (Jude 20)*

The Baptism of the Holy Spirit overcomes our weaknesses. As we strengthen our inner man, the Baptism of the Holy Spirit helps us to overcome any negative patterns in our life:

> *...the Spirit helps us in our*
> *weakness. (Romans 8:26)*

The Baptism of the Holy Spirit enhances a believer's prayer life. The Holy Spirit is a tremendous help in prayer. We can pray with increased spiritual insight when we speak in tongues. Our spirit connects with God in a unique and powerful way:

> *For if I pray in a tongue, my spirit*
> *prays...(1 Corinthians 14:14)*

The Baptism of the Holy Spirit helps us commune with God and pray the unknown. The words we speak are in another language. We may utter words in a known language, but it is foreign to us. Or, we may pray in a heavenly language that only God understands:

> *For anyone who speaks in a tongue does not speak to men but to God. Indeed, no one understands him; he utters mysteries with his spirit. 1 Corinthians 14:2*

The Baptism of the Holy Spirit helps us to pray accurately. How often are we lacking the right words or even the wisdom to pray effectively? The Holy Spirit bridges that gap and makes intercession for us and through us. He prays the perfect will of God:

> *We do not know what we ought to pray for, but the Spirit himself intercedes for us with groans that words cannot express. And he who searches our hearts knows the mind of the Spirit, because the Spirit intercedes for the saints in accordance with God's will. Romans 8:26-27*

The Baptism of the Holy Spirit with praying in tongues is effective in spiritual warfare. When we pray in tongues, we speak directly to God. Our words go straight to the throne room and bypass the enemy:

> *And pray in the Spirit on all occasions with all kinds of prayers and requests. (Ephesians 6:18)*

The Baptism of the Holy Spirit multiplies our ability to praise and worship God. Not only can we pray in tongues, but we can sing in tongues. This is a form of worship where we sing spiritual songs as guided by the Holy Spirit:

> *...Speak to one another with psalms, hymns and spiritual songs. Ephesians 5:19*

The Baptism of the Holy Spirit reminds us we are children of God. Salvation ushers us into the kingdom of God. As his children, the Holy Spirit reminds us we are part of a spiritual family:

> *The Spirit himself testifies with our spirit that we are God's children. (Romans 8:15)*

Obstacles to Receiving the Baptism of the Holy Spirit

Even though the gift is available to everyone who believes, some Christians struggle with receiving it. Many believe that the Baptism of the Holy Spirit is only for special people (the early church or twelve original Apostles). However, the Bible clearly states it is for all believers in all generations. (Acts 2:38)

Others are in fear of receiving something ungodly. They have been taught that "tongues" is of the devil. However, please remember we are not asking Satan for anything; we are directing our prayer to God, our heavenly Father. The Gospel of Luke explains it this way:

> *If you then, though you are evil, know how to give good gifts to your children, how much more will your Father in heaven give the Holy Spirit to those who ask him! (Luke 11:13)*

Insecurity may prevent some from receiving, but, like salvation, it is important to remember that the Baptism, too, is a gift. Simply receive. The Holy Spirit is a gentleman. He never overrides a person's will.

Receiving the Baptism of the Holy Spirit

There are many ways to receive the Baptism of the Holy Spirit. God graciously responds to any spiritually hungry heart who wants more.

I experienced the Baptism of the Holy Spirit upstairs in my bedroom. I was alone and reading the book *The Helper* by Catherine Marshall. At the end of one chapter, there was a prayer to receive the Baptism of the Holy Spirit. I simply repeated the prayer. This was only two weeks after my salvation and I didn't really understand the fullness of what had taken place. But God met me where I was—a spiritually hungry baby who wanted everything God had to give.

Others I know have received the Baptism of the Holy

Spirit during worship, while they were praying, at the altar in prayer, and even driving in the car! I know of a pastor who woke up one night out of a deep sleep and found himself praying in an unknown language!

Some pray fluently in tongues from the start; others begin with a few short phrases and grow into their prayer language or tongues. Everyone's experience is unique!

Here are some basic guidelines when praying for the Baptism of the Holy Spirit, either for yourself or others:

Believe. Any Christian, young or old, needs only to believe that God desires to give them the Baptism of the Holy Spirit. A simple prayer of asking, either led by another or prayed individually, is all that is required. For example:

Lord Jesus, I ask you to baptize me in the Holy Spirit with evidence of speaking in tongues. Thank you for hearing me. I receive that gift right now.

Receive. Instruct the person to maintain an attitude of worship, but anticipate God by waiting upon His presence. Let him or her bask in the presence of the Lord and be filled in his/her inner spirit to overflowing. This is a time to receive from God, not focusing on giving praise to him (see the section "Giving and Receiving"). The person will receive the gift of the Baptism of the Holy Spirit by faith.

Activate the Spiritual Language. Guide the person to use their lips, tongue, and voice to speak what the Holy Spirit directs. He/she must be the one who moves their lips and tongue. Just like speaking a foreign language, the person has control to start and stop the flow, but the Holy Spirit will provide the words. The individual directs the mechanics but not the power or verbiage of the language.

I like to pray aloud with them. I think it diffuses any awkwardness or self-consciousness they might feel. I sense the Holy Spirit filling and the flow rising up and out of their spirit.

Follow up. Rejoice in the answer to prayer and the Holy Spirit's faithful response. You may want to pray until there is a continual flow coming from the person, or until the Holy Spirit directs you otherwise.

Encourage the believer to pray daily in the Spirit increasing the frequency of their prayer over time.

Praying in tongues is a rich and exciting part of a believer's life. As they are faithful to exercise the gift, their prayer language will develop. The result will be an increase in spiritual sensitivity.

Chapter 7
HEALING: THE CHILDREN'S BREAD

Is Jesus able and willing to heal? That same question plagued the mind of a leper who approached Jesus and pleaded, *"If you are willing, you can make me clean."* Jesus answered with words that still ring true today. *"I am willing,"* he said. *"Be clean!" Immediately the leprosy left him and he was cured.* (Mark 1:41)

Healing and healthy living are a part of our covenant with God. From the very beginning, God created a safe and sanitary place for his creation called the Garden of Eden.

But the world we now live in is riddled with sickness, infirmity, and disease. In spite of man's failure to remain in the Garden of Eden, God mercifully provided a means for his children to continue to walk in health

In both Old and New Testaments, God intervened with covenants that presented a pathway to a healthy lifestyle.

Biblical Models for Healing

Under the Law of Moses in the Old Testament, God protected His people by giving them a prescription for healthy living. First of all, He gave dietary regulations which would promote a sense of well-being.

Certain foods and insects were considered "unclean" and forbidden. God also instructed Israel on how to maintain sanitary conditions, and, therefore, limited the infestation and spread of disease. God's insight into a healthy living environment, something foreign to the ancient world, has been scientifically proven to be important in the control of disease today. He shielded His children from sickness and disease by showing them a better and safer manner of living.

In addition, Israel experienced the healing power of God first-hand. They encountered God as *Jehovah-Raphe*, the God who heals, in the wilderness. When Moses led the Israelites by the waters of Marah, the people were parched with thirst and needed fresh, clean water to drink. The waters of Marah were bitter, but God intervened by making them sweet and drinkable. Then He spoke this promise to His people:

"If you listen carefully to the voice of the LORD your God and do what is right in his eyes, if you pay attention to his commands and keep all his decrees, I will not bring on you any of the diseases I brought on the Egyptians, for I am the LORD, who heals you." Exodus 15:26

God demonstrated His divine mercy to heal throughout the Old Testament. Naaman the Syrian was healed of leprosy. (2 Kings 5) Jeroboam's withered hand was restored. (1 Kings 13) The barrenness of Rebekah (Genesis 25:21) and Hannah (1 Samuel 1) was reversed and they bore children. King Hezekiah's illness was healed. (2 Kings 20) The priests were even given jurisdiction to declare the leper and other disease-ridden people cured.

There was no question in the mind of Israel as to whether God healed—he did. King David penned these words in a psalm:

Praise the LORD, O my soul, and forget not all his benefits—who forgives all your sins and heals all your diseases. (Psalm 103:2-3)

Israel believed they served a God who would heal.

But healing in the Old Testament was conditional. According to the covenants of Abraham, Moses, and David, only those who obeyed the law experienced good health and prosperity, while those who disobeyed and sinned against God could expect sickness. Therefore, the Old Testament recorded many illnesses that were the result of waywardness and rebellion.

Whenever Israel sinned and turned from God, they came out from under His protection and curses like illness and poverty would come upon them. (Deuteronomy 28) The plague which destroyed so many Israelites in the wilderness resulted from their dissatisfaction with God's provision and lust for other food. (Numbers 12:33) In addition, King Saul's insanity was caused by unrighteousness. (1 Samuel 17-23, 31)

However, the New Testament sheds a different light on healing. In the New Testament, Jesus combined healing with the preaching of the gospel message. He instituted what we would call "power evangelism" by showing the people God's mercy in the realm of healing.

Consequently, sickness or health was no longer a sign of obedience or judgment. Through compassion and grace, the Son of God cured all diseases. He provided a means for His creation to walk in complete health.

Although healing in the Old Testament was limited to the body of a person, healing in the New Testament embraced more than just physical wholeness. It involved forgiveness of sin, restoration from sickness, breaking the hold of poverty and oppressive social structure, deliverance from demonic oppression, and raising the dead.

The New Testament uses various Greek words to explain the broader sense of the word "healing." *Iaomai*, referred to physical healing (Matthew 15:28), spiritual healing (Matthew 13:15), and healing of the soul. (James 5:16) *Sozo* had a twofold meaning of "to make alive" and "to make healthy." It is the same word translated "to save." The word *therapeuo* was the most commonly used Greek word, which indicated that divine healing was "immediate and brought complete restoration to health." (Matthew 4:23; 8:7) Finally, *apokathistemi* meant "to restore to a former condition of health." (Matthew 12:13)

The key to healing in the New Testament was belief—belief in a God who not only could heal, but would heal. Jairus, a synagogue ruler with a dying daughter, begged Jesus to help her. Even after the servants reported that the child had died, Jesus responded with, *"Don't be afraid; just believe."* (Mark 5:36) This father's faith was the impetus to his daughter's recovery, a healing which raised her from death itself.

Healing also became an integral part of preaching the gospel message. When Jesus sent his disciples out to preach the kingdom of God, He gave them power and authority to heal:

When Jesus had called the Twelve together, he gave them power and authority to drive out all demons and to cure diseases, and he sent them out to preach the kingdom of God and to heal the sick... So they set out and went from village to village, preaching the gospel and healing people everywhere. (Luke 9:1-6)

Finally, just before Jesus ascended into heaven, He spoke his final instructions to His disciples. His parting words, known as the Great Commission, commanded the disciples and future believers to go and preach the gospel to all nations:

And these signs will accompany those who believe... they will place their hands on sick people, and they will get well." (Mark 16:17)

The Book of Acts records the disciple's continued efforts after Jesus ascended to heaven. Peter healed the cripple at the Gate Beautiful (Acts 3:1-10). The apostles continued to heal and deliver, so much so that people put their sick in the shadow of Peter hoping for a cure. (Acts 5:15-16). Stephen did wonders and signs among the people. (Acts 6:8) Phillip healed cripples and paralytics in Samaria. (Acts 8:7)

As his modern-day disciples, we are commanded to do the same. We still have the mandate of the Great Commission to go and lay hands on the sick And we carry the anointing from the same Holy Spirit that empowered the early disciples. There is a mass of hurting people in the world today, and we hold the key to their wholeness. Healing is a part of today's gospel message and a vital part of sharing the good news.

Categories of Sickness

Sickness can be classified as one of four types: spiritual sickness, sickness of the soul, physical illness, and demonic sickness. Although they are categorized and described separately below, they sometimes overlap in their appearance and origin.

Sickness of the spirit. An unsaved person walks in spiritual darkness. Their spirit is damaged, broken and unable to comprehend the things of God. Sin has left a permanent mark on the individual and the light of God is absent or dim at best.

Sin and its effects can also produce a seared conscience. He has become hardened in his response to God. Spiritual darkness overshadows the mind and there is a general lack of awareness of God's presence. The only remedy is salvation, forgiveness, and the infusion of God's life-giving Spirit.

When I became a believer, the curse of sin was broken by the power of Christ. Old ways and habits fell off of me. I had a new perspective and saw the world through different eyes. Faith replaced my unbelief and my entire countenance changed. The life of God pulsed through my veins and my broken spirit was healed. I was alive in Christ!

Sickness of the soul. The soul consists of three parts: the mind, the will, and the emotions. Each of these three parts remain independent of each other, and yet, they are interconnected.

The mind, will, and emotions influence one another in profound ways. Whenever a person is exposed to traumatic events, whether of their own making or inflicted by another, the soul becomes damaged and is in need of healing.

For example, a messy divorce leaves the victim with a broken heart. The mind is tormented with thoughts of rejection. The will is damaged and determined never to be vulnerable again. Healing of the soul is vital to regaining a sense of well-being and the ability to function again in a healthy relationship.

Jesus came to heal wounded hearts. No matter the cause, many suffer with brokenness. They desperately need a deep spiritual healing to right their life. It was one of the mandates of the Messiah that Isaiah foretol:

> *He has sent me to bind up the*
> *brokenhearted... (Isaiah 61:1)*

Research has shown that 80% of physical diseases are linked to damaged emotions. When dealing with healing of the soul, look for these areas that are common trouble spots.

1. Unforgiveness Jesus commanded his disciples to forgive, yet, unforgiveness remains the number one problem associated with healing. Jesus stated it like this:

> *For if you forgive other people when they sin against you, your heavenly Father will also forgive you. (Matthew 6:14)*

Forgiving means to exercise grace, to release, or not hold another in emotional captivity. It carries the connotation of freeing someone from guilt, responsibility, or the consequences of certain actions or inactions. However, forgiveness does not mean that the act was acceptable or did not matter.

Biblical forgiveness is not a feeling, but a choice. It does not accept what happened as being OK. Instead, we choose to place the situation in God's hands and allow him to deal with it. By doing so, we free ourselves from the effects of the sin.

After I invited Jesus into my life, I listened to a series of teachings on forgiving. They were life changing for me. I learned about the power of forgiveness and I chose to release those who had wounded me so deeply. The weight and trauma of my early years disappeared. It was the key to God's restoration and wholeness in my life.

2. Bitterness.

> *See to it that no one misses the grace of*
> *God and that no bitter root grows up to cause*
> *trouble and defile many. (Hebrews 12:15)*

> *Do not judge, or you too will be*
> *judged. (Matthew 7:1)*

When anyone chooses not to forgive, the end result is bitterness. This unrelenting anger and hatred burrows its way deep into the heart. Every small offense is magnified by the bitterness being held within.

Unconfessed bitterness becomes a festering wound that spreads to others. As the situation is retold, anger transfers to others, and new layers of bitterness drive deeper and deeper into the inner man. It is a crippling spiritual condition.

Bitterness also leads to judgment. Just like the law of sowing and reaping, those judgments are like seeds that get planted. Eventually they will be reaped... in the family, a business, or in other relationships.

What if a mother was insensitive to her daughter's feelings? This daughter then grows up resenting the aloofness and judging her mother for it. She judges and grows bitter. Unfortunately,when motherhood arrives, she finds herself acting very much the same with her own children.

The only remedy is to forgive the guilty party. Then ask God to forgive you for harboring these ill feelings and actions. Pray and ask God to uproot the bitterness which was allowed to grow.

3. Hardness of heart

> *Today, if you hear his voice, do not harden your hearts as you did at Meribah (quarreling), as you did that day at Massah (testing) in the desert. (Psalm 95:8-11)*

Intimacy with God and others depends on our ability to open our heart. When situations occur that wound, we put up protective layers that act like a callous. They are hard places in our inner person, insensitive to God and indifferent to others.

Hardness of heart is the fruit of unforgiveness and bitterness. When anyone refuses to forgive and grows bitter, their heart becomes stony and unyielding. The cure is to forgive, repent, and be cleansed by God.

4. Inner Vows

> *But I tell you, do not swear an oath at all: either by heaven, for it is God's throne; or by the earth, for it is his footstool; or by Jerusalem, for it is the city of the Great King...All you need to say is simply 'Yes' or 'No'; anything beyond this comes from the evil one. (Matthew 5:34-37)*

An inner vow is a self-determination that is set in the mind and heart. It is an inner decision that programs actions as well as words. Inner vows actually set walls and borders in a person's life. They are often the root cause of stubborn actions and compulsive behaviors.

For example, a divorced woman may tell herself, "I will never trust another man." This sets up a network of thoughts, feeling, and actions that fulfill that vow. She is bound by her vow to never experience true intimacy again.

The power of the vow ceases by confessing it, breaking the power of it over the person, and praying for release from any habit or influence.

5. Death Wish

When suffering becomes unbearable, many wish for death as a solution to the emotional pain. They entertain thoughts of death or a willingness to die. Although they never choose suicide, a spirit of death overshadows their life.

A death wish must be confessed, broken, and the spirit commanded to leave. In this case, there is emotional healing and deliverance which will covered in the next chapter.

Sickness of the soul can be a complex matter. One prayer will probably not fix every problematic area. As prayer ministers, the best we can do is cooperate with the Holy Spirit and address the specific thing that he highlights for that particular time.

Emotional healing usually occurs over a period of time. As God heals one area, he strengthens the person and then moves on to the next place of concern.

Physical sickness.

> *Jesus went throughout Galilee, teaching in their synagogues, preaching the good news of the kingdom, and healing every disease and sickness among the people. Matthew 4:23*

As Jesus moved throughout Israel, he healed every disease and sickness. The original Greek word for disease is *nosos,* a word meaning malady, disorder, or a specific disease like leprosy

In this verse, the Greek word for sickness is *malakia*, meaning infirmity, disability, weakness, or softness. Jesus healed every kind of problem that the masses presented.

The root of physical illness stems from one of three causes. It may be an organic disorder, a disease like diabetes, heart disease, or cancer.

The physical illness may be a functional disorder. There is a disturbance in the way the body functions, like kidney failure.

And there is physical illness resulting from an

accident. Whiplash from a car accident, a broken leg from a skiing spill, or a torn ACL are examples of this type.

Whatever the source, we are equipped to bring a healing touch. Although physical healing may take place over time, we continue to pray and believe God is at work in their body. Medical care and nutrition are viable and honorable options and additions in this process.

When healing occurs instantaneous, it is usually the gift of miracles or deliverance combined with healing. When Jesus set a woman free from a crippling spirit, she was immediately made well. (Luke 13:10-13)

As we lay hands on the sick, our belief is that they will recover. Our prayer remedy is the "prayer of faith which heals the sick"...

> *And the prayer offered in faith will*
> *make the sick person well; the Lord will*
> *raise him up. (James (5:15)*

Demonic Sickness. This type of illness is a manifestation of a demonic power. The very root of the sickness is an evil spirit. The only remedy for this is deliverance.

When a Canaanite woman confronted Jesus with cries of mercy she said: *Lord, Son of David, have mercy on me! My daughter is demon-possessed and suffering terribly.*

Jesus responded and called healing/ deliverance the "children's bread." He was stating that healing was part of the Israelite covenant. Then Jesus said to her, *"Woman, you have great faith! Your request is granted." And her daughter was healed at that moment.* (Matthew 15:22, 28)

Prayer for Healing

Healings may occur in a variety of ways. A simple prayer of "Lord, please heal this person" can bring wholeness. Other healing manifestations require a period of time for the healing to come forth. Healing becomes a process.

Many find healing by taking the word of God to battle the illness. They proclaim God's promises over the area of illness and see complete restoration.

The gift of healings can be in operation in any of these instances. Healing is as individual as the pain, sickness, or disease that is its cause.

The Holy Spirit reveals and directs prayer for each specific case. Only He knows the real cause of the problem and any side issues that need addressing.

Here is one model for healing prayer:

Step 1: Engage the Person. This answers the question "Where does it hurt?" or "What is the matter?" Listen to the person's answer on two levels.

First, hear on the natural level. What are they actually saying? Second, hear on the supernatural level. What is the Holy Spirit saying about this condition?

Step 2: Diagnose the Problem. This concerns making a diagnostic decision or identifying and clarifying the root of the person's problem. Again, allow the Holy Spirit to guide you to the truth. This step answers the questions:

- Why does this person have this condition?

- Is it a generational illness passed down from his or her family?

- Was there any natural cause for the problem like an accident?

- Has this person been exposed to the occult and is under the influence of a demonic spirit?

Step 3: Determine How to Pray. "What kind of prayer is needed to help this person?"

The healing minister can use one of two types of prayer.. The first is a petition to God, asking him for healing. "Lord, will you please heal this person of diabetes?"

The second type of prayer is a prayer of command. The minister of healing speaks specific words given by the Lord to the area of healing. This prayer involves using your God-given authority to speak to the illness, and the faith to believe that your words are effective.

"I speak to the kidney and command it to function according to God's design."

Step 4: Pray. The prayer minister will lay hands on the person, preferably close to the site of illness. You may ask the person to put his or her own hand on the area and then cover it with your own.

The Holy Spirit may highlight a certain body part, show you something blocking the healing, or direct your actions and words in a particular way. Follow his lead as the gifts begin to operate. If others receive direction from the Holy Spirit, allow their input to guide the ministry time.

There are often manifestations of God's healing power in action. These include shaking and trembling, falling over, body writhing and distortions, laughing and sobbing, prolonged and exuberant expressions of praise, drunkenness, and the effects of past hurts.

Please note: physical manifestations are not necessarily an indication that God is at work. Nor do the lack of manifestations mean that God is not at work! I have seen people walk away from the altar very quietly and then come back days later and tell me how wonderfully God touched them.

Pray according to the direction of the Holy Spirit.

This may as simple as saying "Be healed in the name of Jesus."

Step 5: Rejoice and Encourage. Rejoice with those who are immediately healed. Reassure others who are not instantly healed that God is still at work in their body.

Everyone should walk away assured that God loves them and is working in their life. Encourage them to continue to thank God for their healing and believe for it to manifest.

Sometimes healing takes place over time and often a series of healing prayers are needed. Encourage the person to meditate on healing scriptures.

Healing is an essential part of the gospel message. Rely on the Holy Spirit to directs your prayers and guide the healing process. Always allow Him to lead and trust that He will work with you as you stretch forth your hands to heal.

Chapter 8

DELIVERANCE: FREE INDEED!

Jesus did not limit his ministry to the proclamation of the gospel. It also was marked by a demonstration of his divine authority through healing, miracles, and especially deliverance.

During the earthly ministry of Jesus, approximately one-fourth to one-third of his acts confronted demons or dealt with demonic possession. He cast out demons causing sickness, mental disorders, and commanded their obedience to him in all matters.

Christ operated with authority over the demonic realm, and he taught his disciples to continue in what they had seen him do:

As you go, preach this message: 'The kingdom of heaven is near.' Heal the sick, raise the dead, cleanse

*those who have leprosy, drive out demons. Freely
you have received, freely give. (Matthew 10:7-8)*

The final words in Mark's gospel reiterate this
commands of Christ. Part of each disciple's duty
included dealing with demonic powers:

*And these signs will accompany those
who believe; In my name they will drive
out demons; (Mark 16: 17)*

Like the first disciples, we are also charged with
proclaiming the kingdom of God. We demonstrate
God's kingdom through healing the sick and casting
out demons.

Much of Christianity shies away from the topic of
demons. However, as the occult and false spiritual
practices abound, it is vital that we look at this often
misunderstood ministry.

Fallen Angels

God created Lucifer, or "Light-bearer", to serve and
love him. According to scripture, Lucifer's job was
to shed light and glory onto the presence of God, but
pride intervened and Lucifer became dissatisfied with
his position. He led a rebellion against God and the
result was his expulsion from heaven:

How you have fallen from heaven, O morning

star, son of the dawn! You have been cast down to the earth, you who once laid low the nations! You said in your heart, "I will ascend to heaven; I will raise my throne above the stars of God; I will sit enthroned on the mount of assembly, on the utmost heights of the sacred mountain. I will ascend above the tops of the clouds; I will make myself like the Most High." But you are brought down to the grave, to the depths of the pit. (Isaiah 14:12-15)

Demons are God's angelic beings who sided with Satan to overthrow the throne of God. War among the angels ensued, and Lucifer and his angels were defeated. They received the same punishment as Lucifer—expulsion from heaven. Their main focus now is to kill and destroy mankind, God's ultimate creation.

I do not want to spend much time focusing on demons and their activity. However, for the sake of learning, here are a few of the characteristics of demons:

1. They have intelligence. (Acts 16:16-18; 19:15-16)

2. They are spirits. (Matthew 8:16; 12:43-45; Luke 10:17; 24:39; Revelation 16:14)

3. They manifest themselves in different forms. (Revelation 9:1-12; 16:13-14)

4. They are malevolent. (Acts 19:13-16)

5. They know their own end. (Matthew 8:29; 25:41; James 2:19)

6. They can exhibit supernatural strength. (Matthew 12:29; Mark 5:4; Luke 8:29; Acts 19:13-16)

7. **They must bow to the name of Jesus.** This is always the most important thing to remember! (Matthew 8:28-34; Mark 5:7; Luke 8:26-33)

Effects of Demonic Influence

Evil spirits affect us in three ways: temptation, opposition, and demonization. Temptation occurs when there is a struggle between the flesh and our spirit. Even Jesus experienced temptation in the wilderness when Satan appeared to him.

Opposition comes in the form of an attack, either spiritual, mental, or physical. It includes, but is not limited to sickness, relationship trouble, accidents, mental oppression, or many other negative and destructive situations.

Demonization occurs when an evil presence gets a hold on someone's personality or physical life. Some forms of demonic bondage are the result of habitual patterns of temptation or moral weakness.

Can Christians be "demon possessed?" The answer to this dilemma can be found in the original context of the Greek word *diamonizomenoi*.

This word has been translated in most Biblical texts as "demon possessed." However, the original meaning should be translated "being demonized," "to have a demon," or "vexed, bothered, or harassed."

Two things may be noted in reference to these translations. First, ownership was not a part of the original thought. The word "possession" was added by the translators and assumed to be accurate.

Second, with a new understanding of the term, we can eliminate the confusion regarding the nature of demonic activity. This is not a struggle for ownership, but rather a vying for control. Our new understanding removes the stigma of a believer being "owned."

Mild demonization would vary from harassment to extreme forms of bondage. This could include lying, hardness of heart toward the gospel (2 Corinthians 4:4), apostasy, doctrinal corruption (1 Timothy 4:1; 1 John 4:1-30), and indulging in sinful behavior. (2 Peter 2:1-12)

An example of severe demonization is found in Mark 5:1-10. Jesus delivered a man wandering in the area of the Gadarenes. Distinguishing features of this degree of demonization include:

- The demonic influence is strong, but a person still holds some control over their own life.

- Demons exhibit their control periodically with manifestations like screaming or rigidity.

• Evil spirits may dwell in the person, taking almost complete control.

• A severely demonized person can exhibit supernatural strength.

• The person may project a new personality. The demon can speak through the person it inhabits.

• The demonized person has a strong resistance and opposition to Jesus.

• The afflicted person can convey knowledge previously unknown to them.

• The demonized may speak with languages other than their own (not tongues!)

• The person may be marked by moral depravity.

Demons can gain entrance into an individual's life in a variety of ways. Personal sin is one avenue. Involvement with the occult (witchcraft, contacting the dead, fortune telling) is another and especially prevalent in our society today. Sins committed against the person, like many forms of abuse, can also open the door to demonic influence.

Iniquity and Generational Sin

Another source of demonic activity is a familiar spirit These type of spirits are typically linked to a family and transfer from one generation to the next.

The Bible refers to this as iniquity. It is mentioned over 330 times throughout the Bible. Iniquity differs from sin in that it involves generational issues, those negative actions and characteristics that ensnare a family. The familiar spirit is the root of this behavior and joins with family members to exert its influence. The result is the same...a particular sin manifests in generation after generation.

We can see iniquity working in the life of the Patriarchs in the form of deception. Abraham lied about his wife Sarah to Pharaoh. He called her his sister in order to protect himself. (Genesis 12:11-20) Again, we see he repeated the very same sin with Abimelek in Genesis 20.

His son Isaac does the same with his wife Rebekah. He lies to Abimelek and says Rebekah is his sister in order to protect himself (Genesis 26:7-11).

Isaac's son, Jacob, continues this sin of deception, in fact his very name means "deceiver!" Jacob tricks his father into giving him the blessing intended for his brother Esau (Genesis 27). It is not until Jacob wrestles with God that his name is changed and the curse is broken. (Genesis 32:22-28)

The first step toward deliverance from generational issues is to recognize it. Look for a pattern throughout the generations. If Grandpa had an anger problem, Dad loses his cool easily, and this person struggles with his anger getting out of control, you can suspect a familiar spirit.

Once you recognize the source of the problem, you can now deal with it. Here are my suggestions for breaking free from a familiar spirit:

- Reverse the curse of sin by naming it and declaring that the name of Jesus breaks its power:

Christ redeemed us from the curse of the law by becoming a curse for us, for it is written: "Cursed is everyone who is hung on a pole." (Galatians 3:13)

- Ask Jesus to cleanse the sin with his blood. The blood of Jesus Christ is greater than the blood of the generations.

- Declare and believe that the power of the cross destroys the effects of the sin.

- Command any influencing spirit to depart in the name of Jesus.

Now, proclaim a blessing over the person and family with regard to the sin. If he or she has struggled with anger, bless the family with peace of mind and heart. Encourage the person to meditate on scriptures that will renew their mind to the truth.

The Occult

The word "occult" is generally associated with secret knowledge and practices that deal with the supernatural or psychic phenomena. These are often chosen for the purpose of obtaining personal power. Many occult practices rely on demonic spirits to achieve their goals.

Throughout the Bible, God warned his people about idolatry, sorcery, and witchcraft. He made it very clear that these practices were not to be a part of a holy nation:

Let no one be found among you who sacrifices their son or daughter in the fire, who practices divination or sorcery, interprets omens, engages in witchcraft, or casts spells, or who is a medium or spiritist or who consults the dead. Anyone who does these things is detestable to the LORD; (Deuteronomy 18:10-12)

When the Apostle Paul preached the gospel in Ephesus, many who had participated in the dark arts responded by confessing their actions. They further distanced themselves from the evil by destroying the scrolls that were used:

...they were all seized with fear, and the name

of the Lord Jesus was held in high honor. Many of those who believed now came and openly confessed what they had done. A number who had practiced sorcery brought their scrolls together and burned them publicly. When they calculated the value of the scrolls, the total came to fifty thousand drachmas. In this way the word of the Lord spread widely and grew in power. Acts 19:17-20

Contact with the occult is an open door to evil spirits. Whenever someone entertains the dark arts, they essentially issue an invitation for demonic spirits to enter their life.

What are some of these areas that are entryways to demonic forces? Any action, vow, or participation which seeks a source other than God is considered off limits. This includes horoscopes, fortune telling, psychics, chantings, vows, candle burning, games like the Ouija Board and Dungeons and Dragon, witchcraft, spells, spirit guides, tarot cards, blood sacrifices, and paranormal activity to name a few. Where the occult is found, demonic influence follows.

General Deliverance Prayer

Whenever you minister, look for distinguishing signs of demonic influence. These would include compulsion or the inability to change over a period of time; personal conviction that demonic activity is present; a feeling of being uncontrolled or all tied up inside emotionally; weird or unexplainable manifestations like "magical" abilities.

If deliverance is necessary, authority in Christ is the key (see Chapter 3). However, using your authority does not mean raising your voice or engaging in a screaming match with the spiritual entity. Deliverance can be effective using a calm voice with confidence in your authority.

Whenever a group is praying for an individual's deliverance, only one person at a time should lay hands or speak directly to the person. Too many voices bring confusion to the ministry. Many voices dilute and confuse the strength of your authority. Authority must be clear.

The following examples are suggestions for deliverance prayer. Remember, there is never only one method. You must rely on the Holy Spirit to direct you, especially in areas of deliverance.

Begin by looking the person in the eye (the eyes are the window to the soul.) Keep your eyes open as you minister. This is a form of protection which will give you additional input throughout the process. You may notice a manifestation of the demonic power, a change of facial expressions, or be able to discern when its influence has left.

Should you touch or lay hands on a person receiving

deliverance? There is no absolute in this area. Sometimes it is necessary; other times you will be restrained by the Holy Spirit.

Once ministry begins, the actual process and prayer for deliverance has several definitive components. These include:

Repentance. Any sin associated with this spirit must be cleansed through confession and then asking God's forgiveness. I once heard a minister say, "if you remove the garbage, the flies disappear." Be sure repentance is part of the deliverance process.

Renouncing the demonic activity. The individual should renounce the presence and influence of the demon. This is especially important in the area of the occult. Renouncing involves recognizing the area of sin, choosing to depart from it, and submitting the person's will to God. *Submit yourselves, then, to God. Resist the devil, and he will flee from you. (James 4:7)*

Prayer. If possible, identify the spirit by name (for example, the spirit of fear). The person may indicate what he or she is struggling with. Or the prayer minister may discern a spirit through the gifts of the Holy Spirit.

How can you address a demonic spirit without alarming the person? One way to deal with this problem is to describe the spirit as a "negative or dark force" instead of a demon. Explain that the force has attached itself to the person. While many cannot fully understand the term demonic spirit, they will usually acknowledge a negative force working against them.

Do not embarrass the person receiving ministry by loudly exposing their problem to others. In most cases, deliverance is a straightforward command for the demonic influence to depart.

We cast spirits out with the authority of "the name of Jesus" not our own. *Every knee must bow and every tongue confess he is Lord! (Philippians 2:9-11)*

This is not a prayer of petition asking God to intervene; it is a prayer of command in the authority of Jesus. Confidence in your position in Christ is a must:

• Command the demon to depart and remove its influence from the person.

• Command the root of its influence and any fruit it has born in the person's life to be destroyed.

• Cancel the demon's assignment against the individual.

• Pray to close any open spiritual doors to the demonic influence.

• Pray that the demon would depart without harm to the individual, their family, property, possessions, and without disturbance.

The person ministering may sense when the demon leaves through discerning of spirits. He or she may also note changes or get affirmation from the one receiving deliverance.

After the demonic spirit departs, it leaves a void in the individual's life that must be filled. Pray for the baptism of the Holy Spirit and a fresh filling of the Spirit of God in that area. For example, if the stronghold of fear was broken, ask God to fill the person with peace.

Encourage the person in their walk with God. If he has not accepted the Lord, ask him to join you in a prayer for salvation. Then instruct him to destroy all materials connected to the demonic oppression (occult or pornography, etc.).

After Effects

Deliverance can be as simple as addressing the spirit and commanding it to go, or it may involve a more lengthy process. Much of this depends on the will of the person and their determination to be free, the degree to which the spirit has had influence, and sometimes hidden trauma that may have been an opening for its initial contact. While healing and deliverance often go hand in hand, the end result of true deliverance is freedom:

It is for freedom that Christ has set us free. Stand firm, then, and do not let yourselves be burdened again by a yoke of slavery. (Galatians 5:1)

Chapter 9
THE BLESSING

EACH of us has an innate need to find acceptance. Ideally, we receive this nurturing touch from our family when we are children. Moms and dads demonstrate their love, speak words of encouragement, and actively guide their son's and daughter's growth. Their small acts of love and kindness build a network of security and self-acceptance within the child.

However, not everyone is so fortunate. Many struggle with feeling accepted their entire lives. A part remains unfulfilled and longs for parental recognition.

As prayer ministers, we can fill this inner need by releasing God's goodness. We have the opportunity to be a substitute for missing parents and speak God's words of blessing into a heart.

Blessings also serve a spiritual purpose. Just like

125

these important words nurture children in earthly relationships, they build a bridge to our heavenly Father. A blessing cements the relationship between God and his children and fortifies our spirit.

Biblical Precedents

Why is the blessing important? We can look to the Bible and see that God repeatedly used the blessing to nurture and guide his people.

On the sixth day of creation, God blessed the male and female he had made. He expressed his joy in their creation and the future relationship they would share with him. It was part of his plan for humanity:

> *God **blessed** them and said to them, "Be fruitful and increase in number; fill the earth and subdue it. Rule over the fish in the sea and the birds in the sky and over every living creature that moves on the ground." (Genesis 1: 28)*

Both the Old and New Testaments are filled with examples of older generations reaching out to younger ones with God's words of life. Melchizedek blessed Abraham. (Genesis 14:19-20) Moses blessed the nation of Israel. (Deuteronomy 33:1-5) Israel blessed his son Joseph, his two grandsons Ephraim and Mannassah, as well as his other eleven sons. (Genesis 48-49) Jesus placed his hands on children and blessed them. (Matthew 19:13-15)

The Lord also charged the Levitical priests to bless the people of Israel. They were to speak words over them and attach the Lord's favor and goodness to them:

> *Aaron was set apart, he and his descendants forever, to consecrate the most holy things, to offer sacrifices before the LORD, to minister before him and to **pronounce blessings** in his name forever. (1 Chronicles 23:13)*

God told Moses to have Aaron and his sons bless the Israelites. He even gave him specific words to repeat when Aaron blessed the nation. By releasing these phrases over the Israel, the priests placed the name of *Jehovah* on his people. God entered into a covenant to watch over and bless them:

> *'The LORD bless you and keep you; the LORD make his face shine on you and be gracious to you; the LORD turn his face toward you and give you peace.'*
>
> *So they will put my name on the Israelites, and I will bless them. Numbers 6:24-27*

How to Release the Blessing

In their classic book *The Gift of the Blessing*, Gary Smalley and John Trent define the blessing as having several major elements. These include a meaningful touch, a spoken message attaching high value on the person being blessed, a promise of a special future, and a commitment to fulfill the blessing.

When the blessing occurs within the confines of a family, the blessor has greater opportunity to interact with all these elements. They can oversee and nurture the special words.

However, when we pray with strangers, it is often a one-time occurrence. We do not have a time frame long enough to oversee the fulfillment of the blessing.

Although we may not have that kind of long-lasting relationship, we can still release God's affirmation and acceptance. We may not be able to cultivate the seed, but we can be the ones to plant it. He will do the rest.

These are three elements to include when blessing a person:

Connect. The act of touching a person communicates warmth, acceptance, and affirmation. Laying on of hands is one physical way to meet this need.

We can also connect to the person by looking them in the eye as we bless them. Scripture tells us that the eyes are the window to the soul. As we bless and peer into their open soul, we plant the seeds of life deep within.

Bless. With a loving tone, speak words, scriptures, and any specific revelation that the Lord gives. You may end the prayer with Aaron's blessing that he spoke over Israel (Numbers 6:24-27).

Affirm. We can affirm the blessing of the Lord by making a heartfelt gesture. Shaking hands along with a loving facial expression is one way. A hug is appropriate in many circumstances. We can be affectionate, but not overzealous. Do not overstep any personal boundaries in your enthusiasm.

A blessing brings significance. It feeds the soul and nourishes the spirit. Our simple words can alter the direction of a person's life or fill in a gaping hole.

A Personal Blessing

My parents were like so many others. They probably didn't realize the vital role that a blessing can have in a child's life. But my grandmother understood. I can still remember her blessing me one afternoon right before her death. What a precious memory I have of her and how that touched my soul.

Since then, both my husband and I have blessed our children and grandchildren. We have asked Paul's father to bless him, our daughters, and granddaughters. As a believer, Carl was more than willing to do this and seriously prayed about what to say. His kind words will echo in the lives of the family and leave a legacy of love.

Blessings can be life-changing! Our words of life bring health that flows straight from the throne of God.

Chapter 10
THE ADVENTURE BEGINS

Are you ready?

God is waiting for you to get actively involved.

People are his mission. Hurting, oppressed masses who are hopeless and await his loving touch. They are ignorant that there is a compassionate God who wants to care for them.

You are now prepared to be his ambassadors outside of the church walls. Because you have taken the time to prepare, to learn, and to practice godly precepts and practices, it is now time to engage the world at large.

And you are READY!

The information in this book has equipped you with the basic skills and foundational knowledge to minister on behalf of God. Usher lost souls into the Kingdom of

God. Equip believers with power and a new sensitivity through the Baptism of the Holy Spirit. Heal the sick and deliver the oppressed. As you begin to act on your faith, I believe God will go with you and meet the needs of many struggling people.

Ministry is intended to be a blessing for both the giver and receiver. We are called to demonstrate the Kingdom of God by walking in the grace and power of our example, Jesus Christ. His life was a life of prayer and constant communion with the Father. He walked in the anointing of the Holy Spirit and loved the people whose lives he touched:

...how God anointed Jesus of Nazareth with the Holy Spirit and power, and how he went around doing good and healing all who were under the power of the devil, because God was with him. (Acts 10:38)

God is asking us to continue his work in this fallen world. We have a message and the means to point the way into the Kingdom. He asks us to be like his son, who went about doing good because God was with him. He is also with us.

If you are ready to impact your world, here are a few final suggestions to remember:

Be prayerful. Ask God to give you opportunities to use your gifts and training. Pray for God-given, divine assignments on a daily basis.

Be prepared. Spend time each day filling your spirit through godly practices...pray, fast, read the Bible, worship, and fellowship with other believers. The Apostle Paul told his son Timothy to be instant in season and out of season. (2 Timothy 4:2)

Be ready. Anticipate encounters that will bring glory to God. Be watchful and sensitive to the Holy Spirit. Let him guide you to places and people who are ready to experience his mighty touch.

Be faithful. This is our highest call. If we are faithful to him when he taps our shoulder and directs us to engage in ministry, he will be faithful to show up every time. It is really all he asks of us. He initiates and we respond.

As we go forth in his name, let us remember that we are his hands and feet on earth. May we bring him glory in all that we say and do!

ABOUT THE AUTHOR

My family is the center of my life! I have been married over forty years to my husband Paul who works in the aerospace industry. We have two daughters, two grandchildren, and a granddog! Paul and I have traveled life's roads together. We enjoy working around the home, golfing, biking, travel, and a good movie...with lots of popcorn!

Since 1998, I have traveled to five continents equipping and encouraging others in leadership development, personal growth seminars, mentoring, and conferences. I served as a pastor, created and administrated three Christian training centers, and mentored rising leaders from around the world.

I hold a Master of Divinity degree from Regent University. My publications include *Established: Seeking God's Plan for Spiritual Growth, Empowered:*

A Practical Guide for Personal Ministry, The Word Became Flesh: Studies in the Gospel of John, 7 Easy Steps to Goal Setting Success as well as a variety of articles.

CONNECT WITH PAM

Thank you for purchasing a copy of this book. I pray for exponential growth as you continue on your spiritual journey!

For more information about my ministry, connect with me on my website at

www.pampalagyi.com

Sign up for my newsletter, download other resources, and become part of my blogging community. For more inspirational material, consider registering for my weekly blog on

www.theleadershipladder.com

And if you are a writer, check out my blog where I provide helpful tips on writing and the field of publishing.

www.theaspiringwriter.com

ESTABLISHED: SEEKING GOD'S PLAN FOR SPIRITUAL GROWTH

Are you experiencing all that God has to offer?

In this first book of the "Foundations of Faith" series, author Pam Palagyi returns to the Book of Genesis. In his original creation, God set up his perfect plan. Discover the five basic elements God gave to mankind and lay a solid foundation for spiritual growth.

FREE Bonus... *Established 30 Day Devotional*

THE WORD BECAME FLESH

In this 8 week, in-depth study of the Gospel of John, Pam Palagyi invites you to enter into the culture and history of New Testament times. Experience the Messiah with fresh eyes and apply those spiritual principles to your own life. The study features:

- The seven 'I AM" statements

- The seven signs of the Messiah

- Enriching historical and cultural background

- Word studies and commentary

- Practical applications

7 EASY STEPS TO GOAL SETTING SUCCESS

7 Easy Steps will help you choose your targets, implement specific actions, and follow through to achieve those goals. After you have completed all 7 steps, you will have in your hands:

An outline of your hopes, dreams, and desires

An overview of your yearly goals

A 90 Day Action Plan to propel you forward.

A healthy and balanced approach to living.

When we can tap into God's plan for our life, all things